LATE PREHISTORIC CULTURAL HORIZONS ON THE CANADIAN PLATEAU

by

Thomas H. Richards and Michael K. Rousseau

Department of Archaeology

Simon Fraser University

Publication Number 16

1987

Burnaby, British Columbia

We respectfully dedicate this volume to the memory of

CHARLES E. BORDEN

(1905–1978)

the father of British Columbia archaeology.

TABLE OF CONTENTS

LIST OF FIGURES

LIST OF FIGURES (continued)

LIST OF TABLES

ACKNOWLEDGEMENTS

For constructive criticism, editorial suggestions, and comments on previous drafts of this paper, we thank Roy Carlson, Knut Fladmark, Brian Hayden, Phil Hobler, and Gordon Mohs (Simon Fraser University); Arnoud Stryd and Steve Lawhead (Arcas Associates); David Pokotylo (University of British Columbia), Ernest Walker (University of Saskatchewan), Brian Smith (University of Alberta), and David Sanger (University of Maine).

We are indebted to Roy Carlson and Phil Hobler for lending their technical expertise, advice, and assistance during the final preparation of this monograph. We also thank Arn Stryd for the use of his printer to prepare the tables.

Knut Fladmark, Brian Hayden, Gordon Mohs, Arnoud Stryd, Stephen Lawhead, David Pokotlyo, R.G. Matson (University of British Columbia), and Randy Bouchard and Dorothy Kennedy (B.C. Indian Language Project) generously provided us with unpublished reports and other data which were very useful for our research.

Tom Loy and Wally Bishop of the British Columbia Provincial Museum, Rick Percy and Andrew Barton of the Simon Fraser University Museum of Archaeology and Ethnology, Ken Faverholdt of the Kamloops Museum, and Ursula Surtees of the Kelowna Centennial Museum gave us access to artifact collections.

We would like to express special thanks to the Secwepemc Cultural Education Society, and Native artist Dave Seymour for permission to use the pithouse village scene that appears on the cover.

We alone are responsible for the content of this monograph, and any errors or shortcomings are to be blamed entirely on us.

LATE PREHISTORIC CULTURAL HORIZONS ON THE CANADIAN PLATEAU

INTRODUCTION AND BACKGROUND

In North American archaeological syntheses, the Canadian Plateau is often either ignored, characterized as identical to the Columbia Plateau, or included with the Columbia Plateau and Great Basin (e.g., "Basin/Plateau"). This situation exists primarily because there are no published archaeological syntheses of Canadian Plateau prehistory. It is hoped that the following culture–historical model for the last ca. 4000 years of Canadian Plateau prehistory will help to ameliorate this problem. We believe this synthetic summary will contribute to a better understanding of the late prehistoric period on the Canadian Plateau, and that it will be useful as a general guideline to structure future culture–historical sequences and provide some measure of chronological control for processual studies.

The approach taken in this synthesis has a somewhat "normative" bent (Binford 1965, 1968) with respect to the manner in which the material cultural data are presented, although many important aspects of cultural systems relating to subsistence and settlement are also discussed. This model is not intended to be a final statement on late Canadian Plateau prehistory, and perhaps future research and theoretical trends may partially, or even radically, change some or all aspects of the integrative framework presented here.

Several key concepts must be defined. First, Plateau refers to the ethno–geographic culture area defined as the *Plateau of Northwestern America* (Ray 1939; Kroeber 1939). It lies between the Rocky Mountains in the east, the great bend of the Fraser River in the north, the Cascade and Coast Mountains to the west, and the California border and Blue Mountains to the south. The Plateau includes all Sahaptin speaking people (except the Modoc), the Upper Chinook, Kutenai, Interior Salish, and the Athapaskan speaking Nicola and possibly the Chilcotin, Carrier, and Sekani (Ray 1939:1–2) (Figure 1). According to Ray, two major cultural sub–areas of the Plateau are the Canadian or northern Plateau, and the American or southern Plateau, divided approximately along the international boundary. A possible sub–area is an "Athapaskan area" of central interior British Columbia, consisting of the territory occupied by the Chilcotin, Carrier, and Sekani. However, Ray had strong doubts that the Carrier and Sekani belong in the Plateau at all, but did suggest that the Chilcotin should be considered part of the Canadian Plateau sub–area.

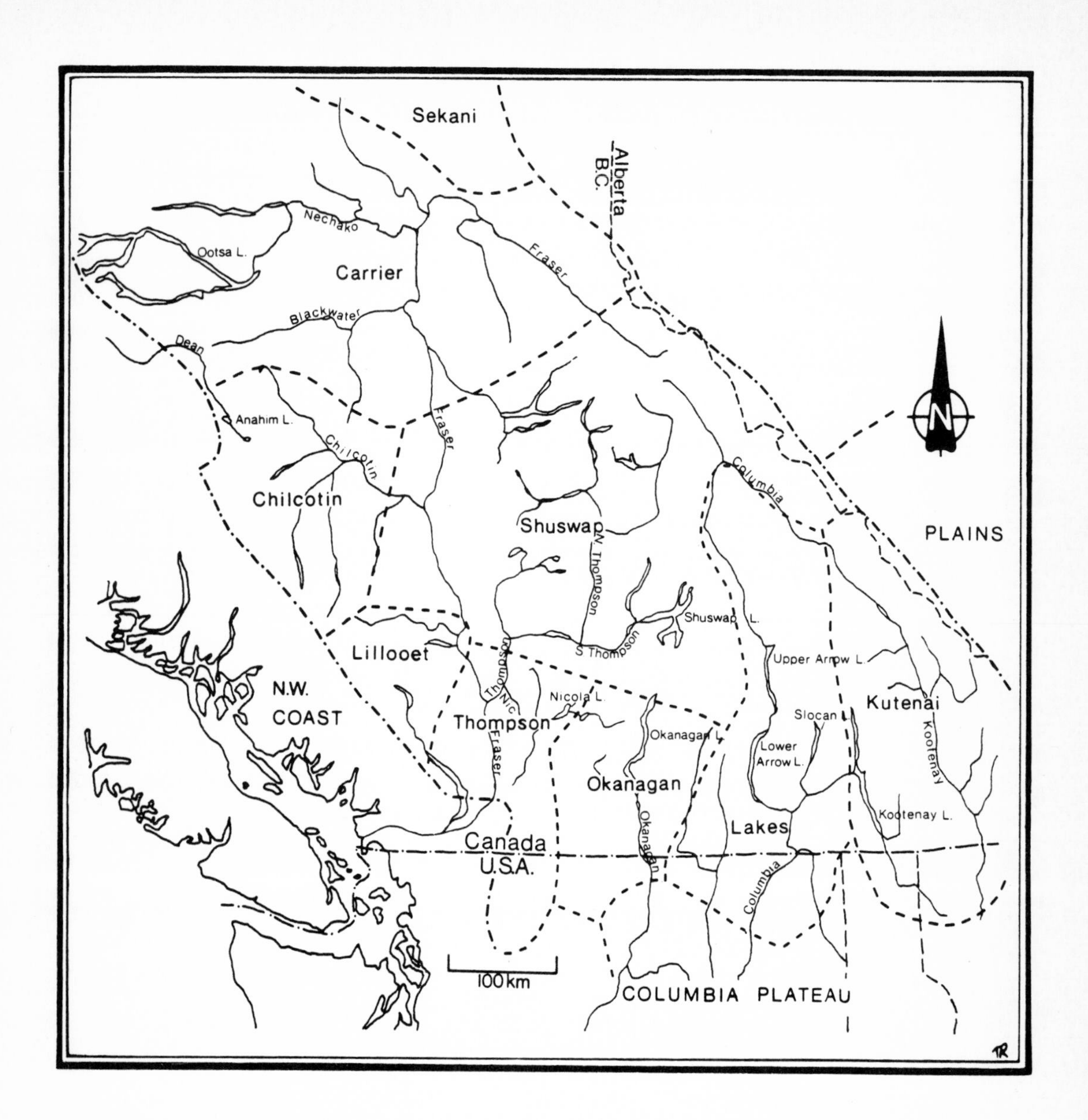

Figure 1. Historic ethno–linguistic divisions on the Canadian Plateau.

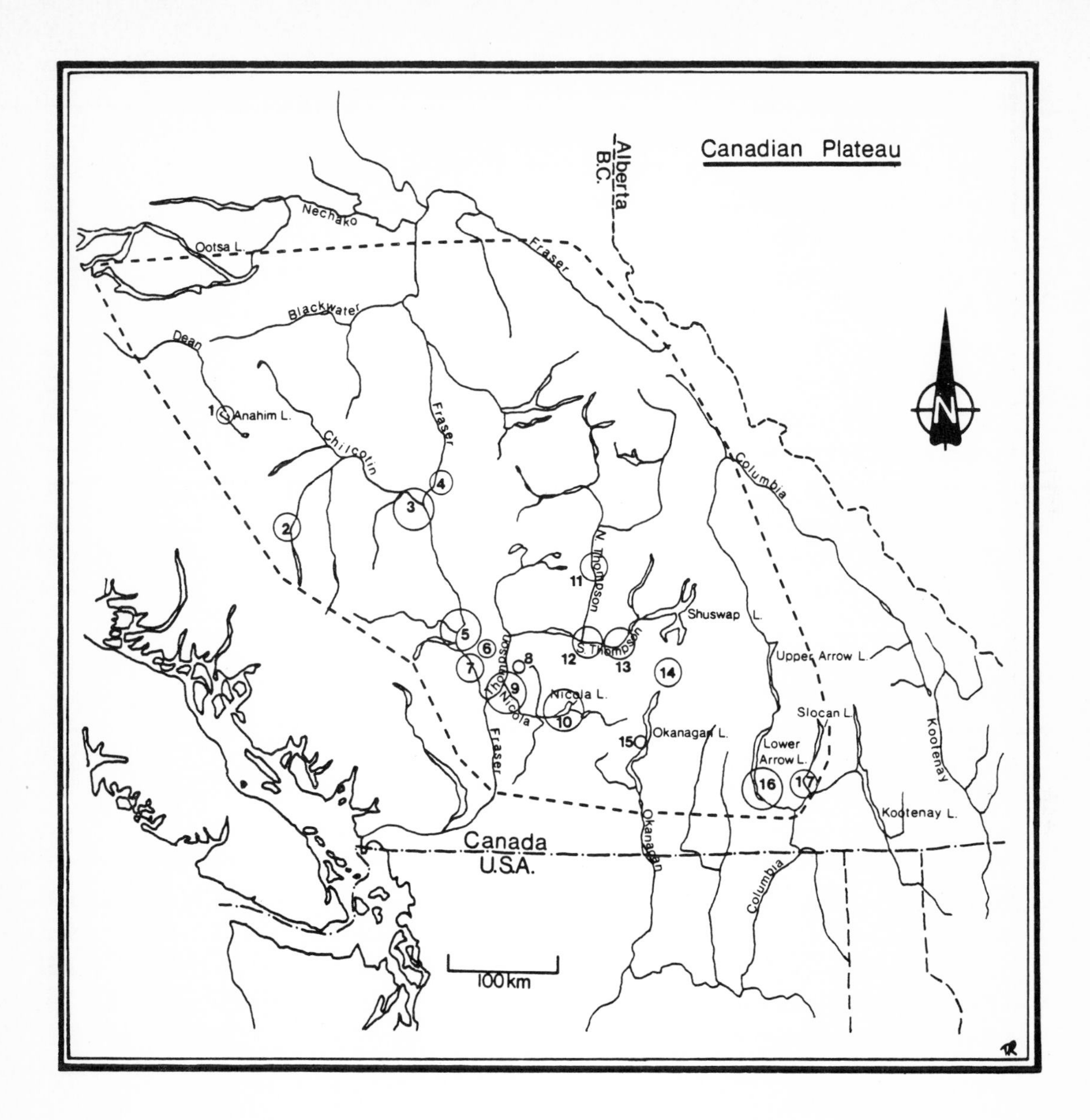

Figure 2. Present estimated extent of the Canadian Plateau cultural sub-area (dotted line), and location of investigated localities (circled). **(1)**: Anahim Lake locality; **(2)**: Eagle Lake locality; **(3)**: Mouth of the Chilcotin River locality; **(4)**: Williams Lake locality; **(5)**: Lillooet locality; **(6)**: Upper Hat Creek Valley; **(7)**: Lochnore–Nesikep locality; (8): Highland Valley locality; **(9)**: Lower Nicola–Spences Bridge locality; **(10)**: Nicola Lake locality; **(11)**: Barriere–Chuchua locality; **(12)**: Kamloops locality; **(13)**: Pritchard–Chase locality; **(14)**: Armstrong locality; **(15)**: Westside locality; **(16)**: Lower Arrow Lakes locality; and **(17)**: Vallican–Slocan Junction locality. References are listed in Tables 1 to 4.

The ethnographic Plateau culture area is widely accepted as an archaeological area (see Willey and Phillips 1958:20). Some of the above sub-divisions of the Plateau are also recognized by archaeologists, with the Columbia (or American) and Canadian (or Interior) Plateaus existing as archaeological *sub-areas* (see Willey and Phillips 1958:20–21). On the basis of available archaeological data, the *Canadian Plateau sub-area* is here considered to consist of the territory in southern British Columbia between the Coast Mountains on the west, approximately 50 km north of the international boundary to the south, and the Rocky Mountains to the east (Figure 2). The northern boundary of the Canadian Plateau is not clearly understood, but it is presently estimated to lie between the Rocky and Coast Mountains along 53° 30' North latitude. It extends approximately 600 km northwest-southeast and 400 km southwest-northeast with a total area in excess of 232,500 square km. We are not presently considering the East Kootenay region (east of the Kootenay River) as part of the Canadian Plateau. Ray's uncertainty about an ethnographic Sekani-Carrier-Chilcotin sub-area of the Plateau is considered to be well-founded, and territory occupied by the Sekani and Upper Carrier is not included in our present conception of the archaeological Plateau area. However, territory occupied by the ethnographic Chilcotin and Lower Carrier is included.

Culture-Historical Integrative Concepts

Archaeological studies in many parts of Canada are still at the stage of constructing culture-historical sequences. Such frameworks are necessary before specific research problems can be properly and adequately addressed within their respective temporal and cultural contexts. Archaeological research on the Canadian Plateau has long been hampered by the lack of a firm culture-historical framework. Sanger's (1969, 1970) sequence for the Lochnore-Nesikep locality was a useful and important initial contribution, however, subsequent research in other adjacent regions indicates that this framework cannot simply be extended to encompass the rest of the Canadian Plateau.

In the following pages we present a culture-historical sequence for the past 3500–4000 years of Canadian Plateau prehistory, and in the process use some terms and concepts which are not widely used—but are definitely not unknown—in North American archaeology. It is important that the reader fully understands the definitions and implications of the following culture-historical descriptive and integrative concepts. Important to the present study is the "tradition" concept, which was in use in North American archaeology long before Willey and Phillips' (1958) attempt at terminological standardization. *The cultural tradition* as proposed by Goggin (1949):

> . . . is a distinctive way of life, reflected in various aspects of the culture; perhaps extending through some period of time and exhibiting normal internal cultural changes, but nevertheless . . . showing a basic consistent unity. In the whole history of a tradition certain persistent themes dominate the life of the people.

Phillips and Willey (1953) accepted both technological and cultural traditions, but later decided the term should be limited to technological traditions only (Willey and Phillips 1958). However, the concept of cultural tradition was not to be laid to rest so easily, and it continued to be used extensively by North American archaeologists, and even eventually by Willey (1966, 1971) in his monumental study of the prehistory of the Americas. His concept of cultural tradition is consistent with previous usage: "Each major cultural tradition is characterized by a definite patterning of subsistence practices, technology, and ecological adaptation" (Willey 1966:4).

To summarize, the salient characteristics of a cultural tradition are as follows: (1) extended temporal persistence; (2) spatial continuity over a large, environmentally distinctive space; and (3) material cultural remains reflecting a unique culture pattern (i.e., subsistence practices, technology, ecological adaptation, social organization, ideology, etc.), although there is culture change within the basic pattern over time (see also Goggin 1949; Phillips and Willey 1953; Caldwell 1958; Lehmer and Caldwell 1966; Willey 1966:4; Bicchieri 1975; Zeier 1982).

Recognition and definition of a specific cultural tradition leads immediately to another problem: how does one make provision for expressing culture change—which can sometimes be substantial—within a cultural tradition (i.e., a distinctive segment of a cultural tradition)? Willey and Phillips (1958) did not define a culture-historical unit which fits the required characteristics of: (1) relatively restricted temporal duration; (2) extensive spatial continuity; and (3) material content reflecting a unique period of cultural stability within a larger cultural tradition. However, one of their concepts has the essentials of these requirements. A *horizon* is described by Willey and Phillips (1958:33) ". . . as a primarily spatial continuity represented by cultural traits and assemblages whose nature and mode of occurrence permit the assumption of a broad and rapid spread." The horizon has the characteristics of relatively short temporal duration and wide spatial extent, although their definition restricts it to single cultural traits or trait complexes. Expansion of the cultural dimension to encompass a temporally restricted segment of an entire archaeological culture (cultural tradition) leads to the *cultural horizon* concept (see Lehmer and Caldwell 1966; Caldwell 1966, 1967; Bicchieri 1975; Zeier 1982; MacNeish 1978; Richards and Rousseau 1983). Just as a *cultural tradition* represents an archaeological culture with considerable temporal duration, a *cultural horizon* represents a unique segment of such a culture. The cultural horizon and cultural tradition are thus interrelated, with the latter comprised of two or more of the former, and the former having no meaning except in reference to the latter.

On a practical level, the cultural horizon is used to group contemporary phases from adjacent localities or regions within an area or "interaction sphere" (see Caldwell 1966; Lehmer and Caldwell 1966; Caldwell 1966; Caldwell and Mallory 1967; MacNeish 1978:65). This is best illustrated in Lehmer and Caldwell's (1966:515) original definition of the cultural horizon concept as:

> . . . a cultural stratum which includes two or more phases, or putative phases, which were approximately coeval and which are characterized by enough common traits, or variants of the same trait, to appear as manifestations of the same basic cultural complex.

They also ellucidate the relationship between cultural horizons, phases, and cultural traditions while discussing their specific case study in the Middle Missouri region:

> In each case the duration of the horizon through time is limited, and in most instances the horizon is found over a considerable geographic area. There is a high degree of correspondence in the cultural content between the phases which fall within each horizon. There is also enough similarity to earlier and/or later phases to demonstrate the persistence of the cultural tradition (Lehmer and Caldwell 1966:515).

The cultural horizon has also been discussed in some detail by Bicchieri (1975:250), although phrased in somewhat more modern terminology:

> To the extent that a horizon represents an extra-regional cultural continuum, it may be considered an "archaeological culture" . . . Being isolated in time to a stationary state, however, it can further be considered as one segment of a larger continuum involving a similar spatial limitation but an expanded temporal dimension. This larger continuum is . . . defined as a tradition in the sense of a "full cultural tradition".

In the following synthesis of late prehistoric Canadian Plateau prehistory, the cultural horizons are cultural-integrative units which document the widespread co-occurrence of several salient cultural traits and patterns that are represented in ***components*** throughout a contiguous geographical area encompassing several archaeological regions within specified, and relatively brief periods of time. Included in this conception is the relatively rapid spread of salient traits/patterns through the interaction of contemporaneous systems (MacNeish 1978) operating in broadly similar environmental contexts. Here, the contiguous geographic area containing contemporaneous interactive cultural systems is the Canadian Plateau sub-area.

We have defined our horizons on the basis of ***components*** rather than *phases* because the definition of local and regional phase sequences has not advanced to the point where horizons can be linked to phase definitions in all regions. It is important to understand that this is not due to a lack of available data, but rather, it is a result of what Canadian Plateau archaeologists have chosen to do with them. Logically, it makes no difference whether phases or components are used, since phases are comprised of components. This approach is not unprecedented on the Plateau, as Caldwell, who originated the cultural horizon concept, defined horizons within the *Southern Plateau Tradition* on the basis of coeval components rather than phases (Caldwell and Mallory 1967:77–81).

Cultural horizons on the Canadian Plateau are conceived as polythetic constructs. Clarke (1968:37) defines a polythetic cultural construct as:

> . . . a group of entities such that each entity possesses a large number of the attributes of the group, each attribute is shared by large numbers of entities and no single attribute is both sufficient and necessary to the group membership.

In the present case, "entities" refers to components. Criteria used to define cultural horizons include approximately contemporaneous inter-regional similarity expressed in: (1) settlement patterns; (2) subsistence modes; (3) winter pithouse size and construction; (4) lithic technology; (5) bone and antler technology; (6) formal artifact attributes; and (7) burial practices. Temporal periods (ca. 1000 to 1500 years) of relative cultural stability expressed by recurring constellations of major traits/patterns are recognized and defined as horizons. The alteration, appearance, or disappearance of several major cultural trait/pattern characteristics at approximately the same time (i.e., over a 100–200 year period) throughout the Canadian Plateau is considered to be indicative of short periods of significant and intensive cultural change. A horizon's appearance within any region may differ slightly in a temporal sense with that of other adjacent regions.

Projectile point types have long been regarded as "type fossils" in Plateau culture-historical research. Such an approach is incompatible with polythetic groups such as cultural horizons. It is clear from the presence of approximately contemporaneous, similar to identical projectile point styles on the Canadian and Columbia Plateaus, Northwest Coast, Rocky Mountain Trench, and Northern Plains, that projectile point types cannot be equated with "cultures" (see also Chance and Chance 1982:411–413). Nevertheless, projectile point styles are excellent temporal markers.

It is stressed that the horizon concept is not intended to replace the "phase" as a culture-historical unit in Canadian Plateau prehistory. Phases are archaeological units of study which are conceived and defined on the basis of similarity in culture traits or patterns which are temporally limited to a relatively brief interval, and spatially confined to a *locality* or *region* (Willey and Phillips 1958:22).

We concur with Pokotylo and Froese (1983:127) that there is a need for systemic regional approaches aimed at examining the full range of aboriginal annual activities, but the first step must be the definition of regional phase sequences. It is recommended that unique sets of phase names be used to define individual regional sequences so that regional differences and research problems can be more readily identified and addressed. Admittedly, this approach will eventually result in a proliferation of regional phase names, however, this system has been used quite successfully on the Columbia Plateau without apparent confusion or major problems.

A Review and Assessment of Previous Canadian Plateau Sequences

The most widely known cultural sequence proposed for the south-central portion of the Canadian Plateau was developed by Sanger (1967, 1969, 1970) for the Lochnore-Nesikep locality in the Mid-Fraser River region (Figures 2 to 5). Considering the lack of detailed comparative information from adjacent regions, Sanger's pioneering work still stands as one of the most comprehensive studies undertaken on the Canadian Plateau. However, if his sequence were to be used as a framework for this synthesis, it would have to be extensively modified. Our approach is to leave the Lochnore-Nesikep sequence as a *local* sequence, as it was originally intended, and to propose a synthesis based on empirical data from throughout the Canadian Plateau.

The Lochnore-Nesikep locality sequence continues to be widely used on the Canadian Plateau in spite of many perceived problems (see Lawhead and Stryd 1985; Lawhead, Stryd, and Curtin 1986; Richards 1978; Fladmark 1982). Three major problems with the sequence are evident.

First, component mixing due to natural, aboriginal, and recent cultural disturbances was extensive at most of the important investigated stratified sites in the Lochnore-Nesikep locality, and resulted in an imperfect interpretation of the prehistoric sequence. Although it can be argued that mixing is a common problem at many sites on the Canadian Plateau, it appears to have been particularly severe at large habitation sites in the Mid-Fraser River region. Available data, and the authors' familiarity with this region indicate that there are relatively few localities suitable for winter pithouse villages that have shelter from the wind, exposure to the sun, access to fresh water, and sufficiently deep and penetratable deposits in which to excavate housepits. Due to the limited number of prime habitation areas, and the suspected high population density in this region during the last 2500

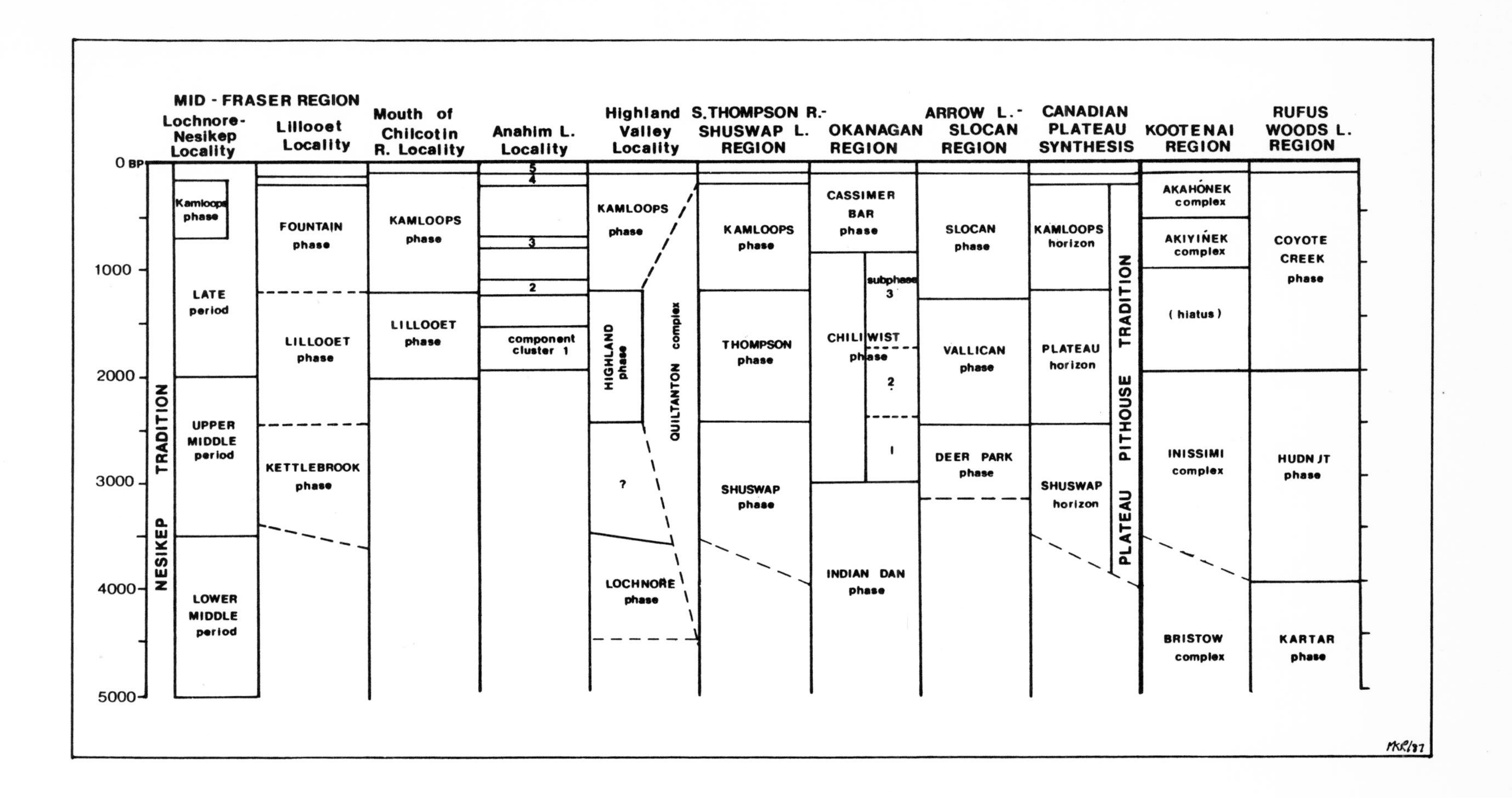

Figure 3. Culture–historical sequences defined for localities and regions on the Canadian Plateau. Recently proposed frameworks for the adjacent Kootenai and Rufus Woods Lake regions are also presented. References are listed in Tables 1 to 4.

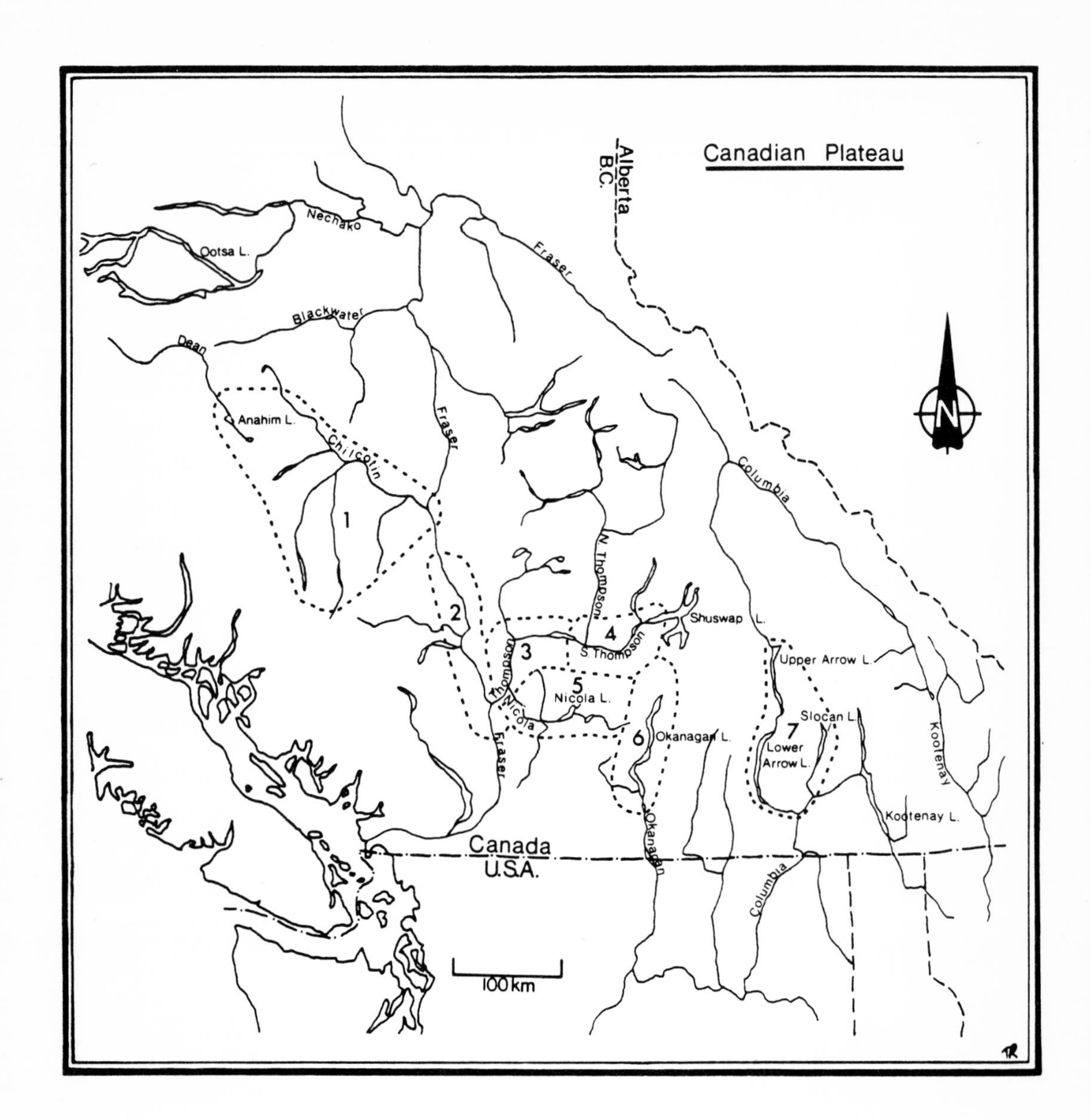

Figure 4. Investigated archaeological regions on the Canadian Plateau. Boundaries are provisionally defined, and may expand if future data allow. **(1)**: Chilcotin Region; **(2)**: Mid-Fraser River region; **(3)**: Thompson River region; **(4)**: South Thompson River-Western Shuswap Lakes region; **(5)**: Nicola region; **(6)**: North Okanagan region; **(7)**: Arrow Lakes region. References are listed in Tables 1 to 4.

years or so, suitable locations for winter pithouse villages were re-occupied many times (see also Blake 1974). Housepit mixing mechanisms recognized by researchers for Canadian Plateau housepits are summarized by Fladmark (1982:123).

A good example of apparent mixing is the Lochnore Creek site (EdRk 7), where a non-housepit component was badly disturbed by later construction of a pithouse on the same spot. The pithouse itself was repeatedly disturbed by re-use (see Sanger 1970:21-28). Another example is the deeply stratified Nesikep Creek site (EdRk 4) which was disturbed by aboriginal pit excavations, possibly including housepits, into earlier components. Inspection of the *Zone VI* floor plan of the main excavation block (see Sanger 1970:Figure 4) reveals the extent of the aboriginal disturbance. Pits excavated from the overlying *Zones III, IV,* and *V* are shown going through *Zones VI* and *VII* to underlying sterile gravel. Aboriginal excavation of a pit from *Zone III* through *Zones IV-VII* would have removed and redeposited cultural materials from the underlying zones on the *Zone III* occupation surface. Thus, cultural material from early components would be mixed with materials from later components on later occupation surfaces, leaving the earliest ones relatively unmixed but disturbed.

A second major problem is associated with the radiocarbon dates used to establish the Lochnore-Nesikep locality sequence. Several dates from the same components are widely divergent, and the validity of many were questioned by Sanger (1970:103-106), which left him with very few absolute dates to structure his sequence. A single sample of charcoal from *Zone I* of the Lochnore Creek site (EdRk 7) produced five dates: 2670±130 BP (GSC 407), 2605±140 BP (GSC 407-2), 3280±125 BP (GX 407), 3220±90 BP (GX 407-2), and 2680±100 BP (I 1866). Ages determined by the Geological Survey of Canada (GSC) and Isotopes Inc. (I) labs were fairly close, however, there is an approximate 500 year difference between these dates and those provided by the Geochron (GX) lab. Dr. H. Krueger of the Geochron lab related that, ". . . it was the most confusing and confounding situation that has arisen in 21 years and 11,000 ^{14}C analyses" (Krueger, pers. comm. 1985). Also, absolute dates were assigned to all excavated components on the basis of their relative stratigraphic position with respect to acceptable radiocarbon dated components (Sanger 1970:Table LV). Many of these dates are now considered to be of dubious accuracy in light of recent research (see Richards 1978; Fladmark 1982:127; Lawhead, Stryd, and Curtin 1986).

Thirdly, recent research indicates that the two cultural traditions outlined for the Lochnore-Nesikep locality (Sanger 1969) were defined prematurely. An over-emphasis on the significance of microblade technology led to the proposal of the *"Nesikep Tradition"*, a 7000 year-long cultural continuum. Convincing evidence for such cultural continuity has yet to be demonstrated, and the commencement date of 7000 BP has not been substantiated in any excavated and dated

Figure 5. The Lochnore-Nesikep locality in the Mid-Fraser River Region, looking north.

Figure 6. The area between Gibbs Creek (lower right) and Pavilion (distant) in the Mid-Fraser River region, looking north.

component on the Canadian Plateau. The reportedly earlier *"Lochnore Complex"* is disputed on the basis of present data that suggest it is not earlier than 7000 BP. The single component from the Lochnore–Nesikep locality attributed to this complex (EdRk 7, *Zone III)* was not radiocarbon dated, and the assemblage contains artifacts (Sanger 1970:Figure 31a,b,n,o) that are strikingly similar to those assigned to the recently proposed *Lehman phase* and *Lochnore phase* components of the Mid–Fraser and Thompson River regions dated between ca. 6000 and 4000 BP (see Lawhead and Stryd 1985; Lawhead, Stryd, and Curtin 1986:160–175).

Subsequent researchers have tended to assume this sequence is valid throughout the Canadian Plateau and have applied it rather uncautiously. The Lochnore–Nesikep sequence resulted from investigations at a single *locality*, and it is methodologically unsound to generalize the prehistory of the entire Canadian Plateau from a single locality. Further, the Lochnore–Nesikep locality is situated on the western periphery of the Canadian Plateau, adjacent to the Northwest Coast culture area, and there are clear indications that prehistoric populations occupying this locality closely interacted with coastal cultural groups, especially during the last 2000 years or so. The apparent degree of interaction is not characteristic of other parts of the Canadian Plateau, and it is hard to imagine a more inappropriate locus from which to generalize about Canadian Plateau prehistory, especially for the late prehistoric period.

In a recent descriptive overview of British Columbia prehistory, Fladmark (1982) is also critical of the Lochnore–Nesikep locality cultural sequence. In addition, he points out that many problems with the interpretation of Canadian Plateau prehistory are the result of most research having been conducted at mixed, multi–component housepit sites. Although Fladmark's overview is a useful introduction to the prehistory of the Canadian Plateau, it is not an integrative synthesis.

A considerable amount of research has been carried out in the Lillooet locality (Figures 2 and 6) of the Mid–Fraser River region in the last fifteen years (Stryd 1972, 1973a, 1974, 1980, 1981b, 1983a,b; Stryd and Lawhead 1978; Hayden *et al* 1986). Several of these projects also encountered problems with component mixing in housepit sites. On the basis of two seasons of fieldwork, Stryd (1973a,b) proposed two distinct cultural sequences which were essentially elaborations of Sanger's Lochnore–Nesikep sequence. While largely based on investigations near Lillooet, these sequences have been used in other parts of the Canadian Plateau. After three further field seasons, a sequence derived from the Plateau Pithouse tradition model (Richards and Rousseau 1982) was proposed for the Lillooet locality (Stryd 1983a, pers. comm. 1986) (Figure 3).

Figure 7. A housepit village near the confluence of the Chilko and Chilcotin Rivers in the Chilcotin region, looking northeast.

Figure 8. The Walhachin locality in the Thompson River region, looking east.

Figure 9. The area at the northern end of Nicola Lake in the Nicola Valley region, looking south.

The late Roscoe Wilmeth spent many seasons excavating in the Anahim Lake locality of the northwestern Canadian Plateau (Wilmeth 1978b, 1981) (Figure 2). Instead of phases, he proposed "component clusters" as a preliminary means of ordering his data (Figure 3). The contents of Wilmeth's component clusters generally agree with our sequence of cultural horizons, although slight differences are evident. These differences may be partially the result of suspected component mixing, but more likely they are related to a late prehistoric proto-Chilcotin migration into the area (Wilmeth 1978b), and adaptation to a relatively salmon-poor environment. More recently, work carried out at Eagle Lake (Matson *et al* 1980; Magne and Matson 1984) and at the mouth of the Chilcotin River (Matson, Ham, and Bunyan 1981) has addressed the problem of late Athapaskan southward migration. For the purposes of temporally ordering the archaeological data, Matson and Magne have adopted Stryd's (1973a) late prehistoric sequence (Figure 3), with the addition of the protohistoric/historic *Eagle Lake phase* (ca. AD 1700–1850), which is thought to represent Athapaskan occupation.

A formal cultural phase sequence for the Thompson River region (Figures 4 and 8) has yet to be defined. The few excavations that have been conducted are reported and discussed using Sanger's (1970) scheme for the Lochnore–Nesikep locality and/or Stryd's (1973a) sequence for the Lillooet locality (e.g., Von Krogh 1978; Whitlam 1980; Pokotylo, Binkley, and Curtin 1987). A regional framework is also lacking for the Nicola Valley.

Lawhead and Stryd have recently conducted investigations in the nearby mid-altitude Highland Valley, which lies southeast of Ashcroft between the Thompson River and Nicola regions (Lawhead, Stryd, and Curtin 1986) (Figure 2). Three late prehistoric culture-historical constructs are defined for this locality: the *Quiltanton complex* (ca. 5500/2100–1000/200 BP); *Highland phase* (ca. 2400–1200 BP); and *Kamloops phase* (ca. 1200–200 BP) (Lawhead, Stryd, and Curtin 1986:183–195) (Figure 3). Highland phase and Kamloops phase sites are interpreted as small hunting camps and stations seasonally occupied by Salishan populations from the lowland river valleys. Quiltanton complex components are approximately contemporaneous with the Highland and Kamloops phases, and are characterized by high frequencies of microblades and cores. Lawhead and Stryd provisionally interpret the Quiltanton complex components as possible evidence for seasonal utilization of this locality by Athapaskan-speaking Nicola-Similkameen people from the nearby Nicola Valley.

In the Kamloops locality (Figures 2 and 10) a late prehistoric cultural sequence attributed to the Nesikep tradition was proposed by Wilson (1980). It has recently been expanded temporally and spatially into a late prehistoric–historic sequence for the South Thompson River-Western Shuswap Lakes region, and is now considered to be affiliated with the Plateau Pithouse tradition (Richards and

Figure 10. The area between Kamloops (foreground) and Monte Creek (distant) in the South Thompson River Valley, looking east.

Figure 11. The Scotch Creek locality (center) on Shuswap Lake, looking northeast.

Rousseau 1982; Rousseau and Richards 1985) (Figure 3). The South Thompson River–Western Shuswap Lakes regional sequence closely corresponds with the cultural horizon sequence proposed in the following pages, although it must be stressed that we have not simply generalized from this region to the entire Canadian Plateau.

For the Canadian Okanagan, Grabert (1974) proposed a sequence of phases originally defined for the Wells Reservoir, located at the confluence of the Okanagan and Columbia Rivers (Grabert 1968, 1970). Subsequent research in the southern Canadian Okanagan (e.g., Copp 1979; Roberts 1974; Rousseau and Howe 1979) confirms that the later prehistory of this area is quite similar to the Wells Reservoir sequence, but these later studies have been hindered by a paucity of radiocarbon dates. Recent excavations conducted by Rousseau (1984a, 1984b) at the Westside locality in the North Okanagan Valley (Figure 2) suggests that the late prehistory of this area has marked similarity with that of the South Thompson River–Western Shuswap Lakes region, and a general resemblance to the Southern Okanagan and Rufus Woods Lake region on the north–central Columbia River (Jermann 1985; Campbell 1985d). Grabert (1974:72) also recognized differences between the prehistory of the northern and southern Okanagan valley and remarked that:

> . . . it should be understood that the northern valley sub–region possesses some qualities distinct from the south; that although the north is not unique, neither is it a carbon duplicate of the Wells Reservoir archaeology. . . . In the final analysis the definition of culture phases in the Okanagan region may show that a mixture of technological traditions is present in the region. This is due in part to the valley's intermediate position between two geographically separate regions which converged culturally in recent prehistoric times. . . . Given that fish played so important a role in the storeable food resource of the Northwestern peoples, dwellers in the Okanagan would have had to look either to the Thompson River–Shuswap Lakes or to the Columbia River to the south for salmon. Thus, some part of their seasonal rounds brought them into socio–economic relationships with southern or northern peoples. Assuming that fishing was important for a substantial time span, it would have been an effective agent in structuring extra–community social relationships for prehistoric Okanagan peoples.

On the basis of Grabert's and Rousseau's research, it is suggested that the North Okanagan Valley should be considered as being aligned with the Canadian Plateau culture sub–area rather than with the Columbia Plateau. The boundary between the North and South Okanagan regions is provisionally recognized as existing at Okanagan Falls (see Teit 1930:199; Rousseau 1984a:157). For now, this locale is considered to be the approximate southern extent to which the Canadian

Figure 12. The Kalamalka Lake (left) and Woods Lake (distant) area in the North Okanagan region, looking south.

Figure 13. Upper Arrow Lake in the Arrow Lakes region, looking north.

Plateau cultural horizon scheme should be applied in the Okanagan Valley. This does not imply that a well-defined break in the continuity or content of the late prehistoric archaeological record exists at this location, rather, there is an observable subtle melding of North and South Okanagan cultural traits and patterns that conform to a cline between Penticton to the north, and Oliver to the south.

In the Arrow Lakes region of the West Kootenays (Figures 4 and 13) Turnbull (1977:107-111;Figures 2,3) defined a preliminary late prehistoric sequence which included the *Deer Park phase* (ca. 3300-2500/1600 BP) followed by the *Late Period* (ca. 1600-200 BP). This sequence has recently been expanded and modified by Eldridge (1984:42-46) in conjunction with investigations at the Vallican site (DjQj 1) in the Slocan Valley (see also Mohs 1982; Rousseau 1982). The revised sequence includes the *Deer Park phase* (ca. 3200-2400 BP), the *Vallican phase* (ca. 2400-1300 BP), and the *Slocan phase* (ca. 1300-200 BP) (Table 3).

Turnbull (1977:112-120), Eldridge (1984:43), and Choquette (1985) have noted that there are similarities between Arrow Lakes region materials with those from Kettle Falls on the Columbia River ca. 100 km to the south (Chance and Chance 1982). Historic and ethnographic accounts suggest that the southern territorial boundary of the Lakes Salish lay at Little Dalles on the Columbia River just north of Kettle Falls, but it is maintained that they visited this area, along with other groups, only during the salmon fishing season in the summer and early fall. When the fishing season ended, the Lakes returned to their homeland in the north (Arrow Lakes region) to spend the winter (Bouchard and Kennedy 1985:25-26). Teit (1930:251) indicates that Eagle Pass between Sicamous and Revelstoke, and "Fire Pass" (Cherry Pass) between Vernon and the upper end of Lower Arrow Lake were travelled by the Shuswap, probably to interact with the Lakes. Thus, the Arrow Lakes region occupies a unique position intermediate between the Canadian and Columbia Plateaus.

Chance and Chance (1982:421) have hypothesized that the Lakes separated from the linguistically-related and more southerly Colville and migrated north to occupy the Arrow Lakes region in relatively late prehistoric times, replacing an unknown group. Their model may have some validity, as Eldridge (1984:43) notes that the latter half of the Slocan phase component (ca. 700/500-200 BP) is quite similar to the *Shwayip period* at Kettle Falls, whereas the inital half of this phase (ca. 1300-700/500 BP) is characterized by slightly different material trait characteristics.

We have some reservation about considering the occupants of the Arrow Lakes region as full participants in the Plateau Pithouse tradition. Arrow Lakes region components express many notable similarities in the nature and temporal distribution of material cutural traits with those elsewhere on the Canadian Plateau (particularly between ca. 3300 and 700 BP), and like the North Okanagan, this region is characterized by an admixture of Canadian Plateau and Columbia Plateau cultural traits and patterns.

Archaeological investigations conducted at late prehistoric sites in the Lower Fraser River canyon region between Boston Bar and the Hope area clearly indicate that this region is very strongly aligned with the Fraser Delta and Southern Northwest Coast regions, although some similarities with the Plateau do exist (e.g., use of winter semi-subterranean dwellings, a roughly similar projectile point sequence and chipped stone technology) (Borden 1961, 1968; Mitchell 1963; Hanson 1973; Von Krogh 1976, 1980; Archer 1980; Eldridge 1982). The occupants of the Lower Fraser in the 19th century were the Upper Stalo or Tait, who were linguistically and culturally affiliated with the Coast Salish groups to the west (Boas 1890:321; Duff 1952:11; Hill-Tout 1903:355). Because of these archaeological and linguistic differences, we do not regard the Lower Fraser River region as participating in the Plateau Pithouse tradition. We consider it as being transitional to, and more strongly aligned with, the distinctively different South Coast region (see also Von Krogh 1980:18).

LATE PREHISTORIC CANADIAN PLATEAU CULTURAL HORIZONS

Consideration of the currently available research data leads us to propose that three cultural horizons existed on the Canadian Plateau between ca. 4000/3500 and 200 BP. Together they comprise the *Plateau Pithouse tradition*, a cultural tradition characterized by semi-sedentary, pithouse dwelling, hunter-gatherer, logistically organized (Binford 1980), band-level societies that relied heavily on anadromous fish for subsistence. The Plateau Pithouse tradition and its constituent cultural horizons were conceived by adopting an empirical approach, utilizing data from virtually every excavated component on the Canadian Plateau. Our many years of excavation and survey experience throughout the Canadian Plateau were also heavily drawn upon. This approach allowed us to recognize broad cultural similarities shared between regions which have not been previously recognized. Caution was exercised when considering components which appeared to be badly mixed, and we occasionally drew conclusions on content and chronology that are somewhat divergent from those of the original investigators.

Our consideration of the currently available regional syntheses and personal experience suggest that several distinctive archaeological regions can be provisionally defined for the Canadian Plateau (Figure 4). They include: the Chilcotin region; Mid-Fraser River region; Thompson River region; South Thompson River-Western Shuswap Lakes region; Nicola region; North Okanagan region; and Arrow Lakes region (Figures 4 to 13). Although these regions share an overall general level of environmental similarity, they are regarded as being separable on a combined consideration of: (1) minor to moderate regional environmental differences with regard to climate, natural resource abundance and distribution (see Palmer 1975: 204–213,228); (2) observed differences in settlement and subsistence strategies/patterns expressed in the archaeological record; (3) geographic isolation imposed by mountain ranges or major rivers; and (4) ethnographically documented linguistic/ ethnic group boundaries.

Formidable geographic obstacles such as major mountain ranges most certainly affected ease of human movement between some regions, consequently hindering inter-regional interaction to some degree. This may have been particularly true of the juxtaposed North Okanagan, South Thompson-Shuswap, and Arrow Lakes regions. Despite natural barriers, the general level of similarity expressed in material culture from excavated sites from these latter regions suggest that some cultural interaction was certainly taking place during the last 3500/4000 years, but the level and intensity of this contact remains poorly understood.

The horizon definitions presented below are intended as guidelines which will be of value in formulating future local and regional phase sequences, and for framing and testing models relating to culture process and adaptation. Once all regional phase sequences have been defined, it is very probable that the horizon definitions presented here will undergo some revision. The horizons will then assume greater value as integrative devices that can be used to assess the level of inter-regional cultural interaction, group mobility, and diffusion of cultural traits and patterns.

SHUSWAP HORIZON

The earliest cultural horizon belonging to the Plateau Pithouse tradition is the *Shuswap horizon,* estimated to have commenced sometime between ca. 4000 and 3500 BP, and ended around 2400 BP (Figures 3 and 14). There are fewer excavated components for this horizon than for the following two horizons (Table 1), nevertheless, they are represented in all regions (Figure 15). Present data indicate that the beginning of this horizon marks the initial use of semi-subterranean pithouses as winter habitations on the Canadian Plateau.

The Shuswap horizon appears to have begun shortly after the onset of cooler and moister climatic conditions around 4500 to 4000 BP (Figure 14) following the warm and dry Altithermal that lasted from about 8000 to 4500 BP (Hansen 1955; Alley 1976; Clague 1981; Hebda 1982; King 1980; Mack, Rutter, and Valastro 1978; Mathewes 1984; Campbell 1985a). Perhaps this cooling trend is responsible for the development of adaptive strategies which differed from those adopted during the Altithermal period (see Lawhead and Stryd 1985; Lawhead, Stryd, and Curtin 1986). Sometime between 3000 and 2000 BP, warmer and drier climatic conditions were established that approximated those experienced today. It is clear that by 3000 BP the Plateau Pithouse tradition adaptive cultural pattern had been established throughout the Canadian Plateau. The majority (68%) of excavated Shuswap horizon components are from housepit sites (Table 1), and therefore, the following descriptions of this horizon's characteristics are biased towards data recovered from this site type.

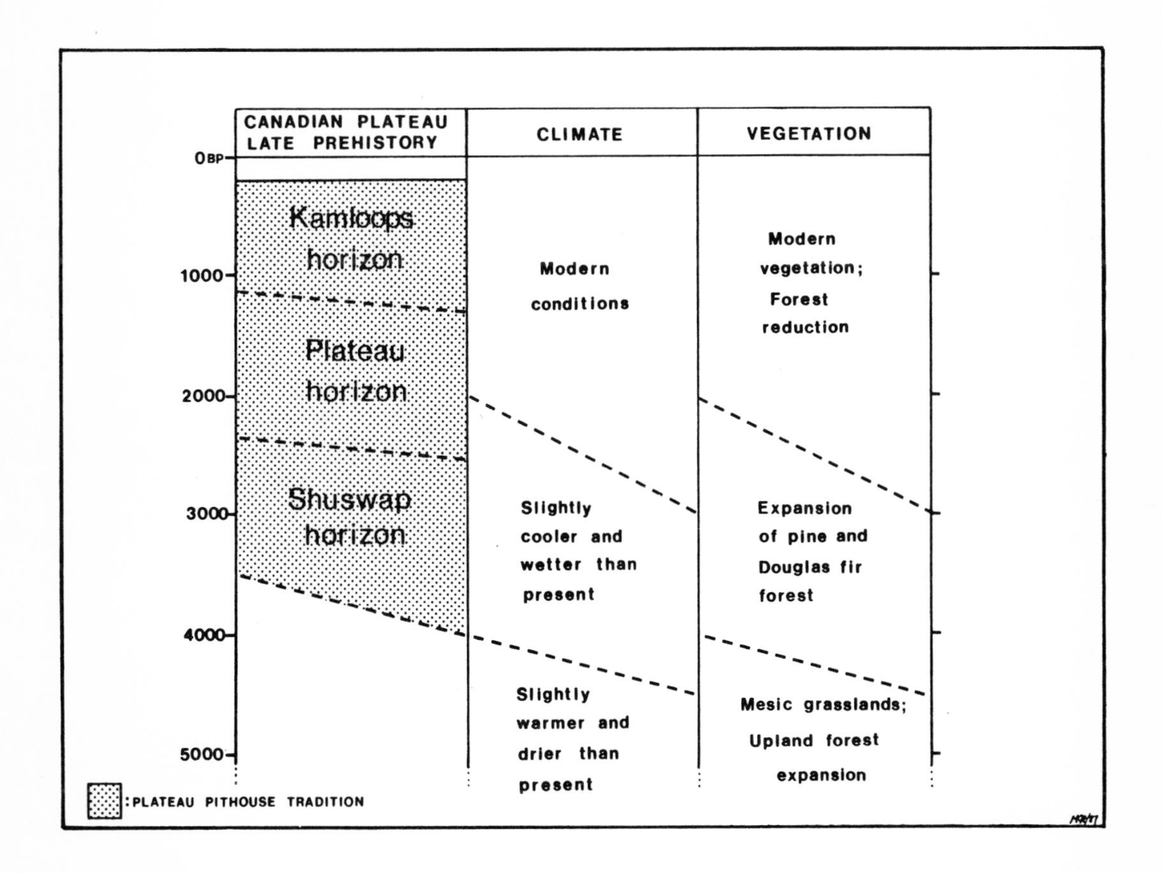

Figure 14. Cultural and paleoenvironmental sequences for the late prehistoric period on the Canadian Plateau.

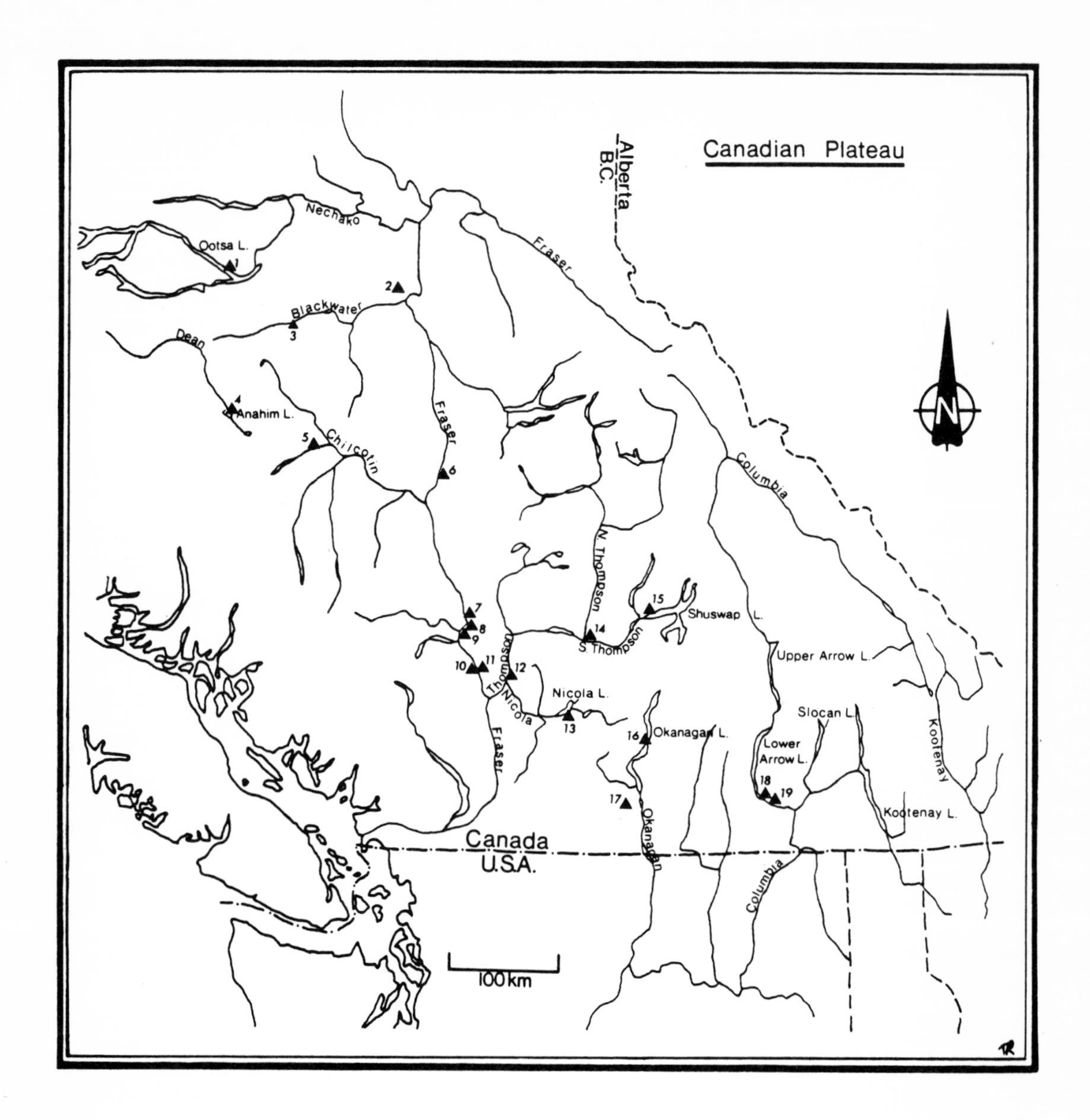

Figure 15. Location of excavated components attributed to the Shuswap horizon. Borden site designations and references are listed in Table 1.

Horizon Characteristics

Surficially, Shuswap horizon housepit depressions are large, averaging 10.7 m in diameter (s.d. = 2.19 m; range = 7.6 to 16.0 m) (see Table 4). They lack raised earth rims, and are circular to oval in plan. Excavations reveal that they are usually flat-bottomed with steep walls, and the floors tend to be rectangular in plan.

Hearth features are common, as are internal storage and cooking pits (earth ovens). Earth roof insulation layers and post-holes have been found, implying substantial wooden superstructures as described by Boas (1890), Dawson (1891:7), and Teit (1900:192–194) for the ethnographic period. Some houses may have had less massive superstructures without earth roof insulation. The sample of excavated houses contain one or two major occupational episodes.

Evidence for a ground level side-entrance is present at site EeRb 10 (Richards and Rousseau 1982:75). Side entrances may have been common, especially on houses lacking substantial roof structures. External storage or cooking pits are rare, and date to the last 500 years of the horizon (see Sendey 1972:11; Mohs 1980a:53; Turnbull 1977:105, Figure 41).

Projectile points display a relatively high degree of stylistic variability (Figure 16). They have a mean length of 4.00 cm, width of 1.80 cm, and an average neck width of 1.10 cm (Table 6), suggesting that they were used to tip spears or atlatl darts rather than arrows (see Corliss 1972; Stryd 1973a:49–50; Thomas 1978; Wilson 1980:44–45). Most of the points are lanceolate or triangular in form. Commonly recurring formal "types" include: (1) a form with shallow corner-removals or side-notches, markedly concave basal margin, and pronounced basal or basal-lateral "ears" (Figure 16a–f); (2) a lanceolate form with a markedly concave basal margin (Figure 16g–i); (3) a form having side or corner removals or shallow notches, pronounced shoulders (some have slight lateral barbs), expanding base, and concave basal margin (Figure 16j–l); (4) a form with a parallel to slightly contracting or slightly expanding stem with well-defined, narrow, rounded shoulders and concave basal margin (Figure 16m–o); (5) a lanceolate form with well-defined, slightly rounded shoulders, slightly expanding stems, and slightly concave basal margins (Figure 16p–r); (6) a form having narrow, rounded shoulders, parallel stem, and straight to slightly convex basal margin (Figure 16s–u); (7) a form with a contracting stem, broad, slightly rounded shoulders, and straight to slightly convex basal margin (Figure 16v–y); and (8) a form with markedly rounded shoulders, slightly expanding stem, and slightly to markedly concave basal margin (Figure 16z–d'). Pronounced lateral barbs are uncommon on Shuswap horizon points, however, towards the end of the horizon small barbs, often only unilateral, are sometimes present.

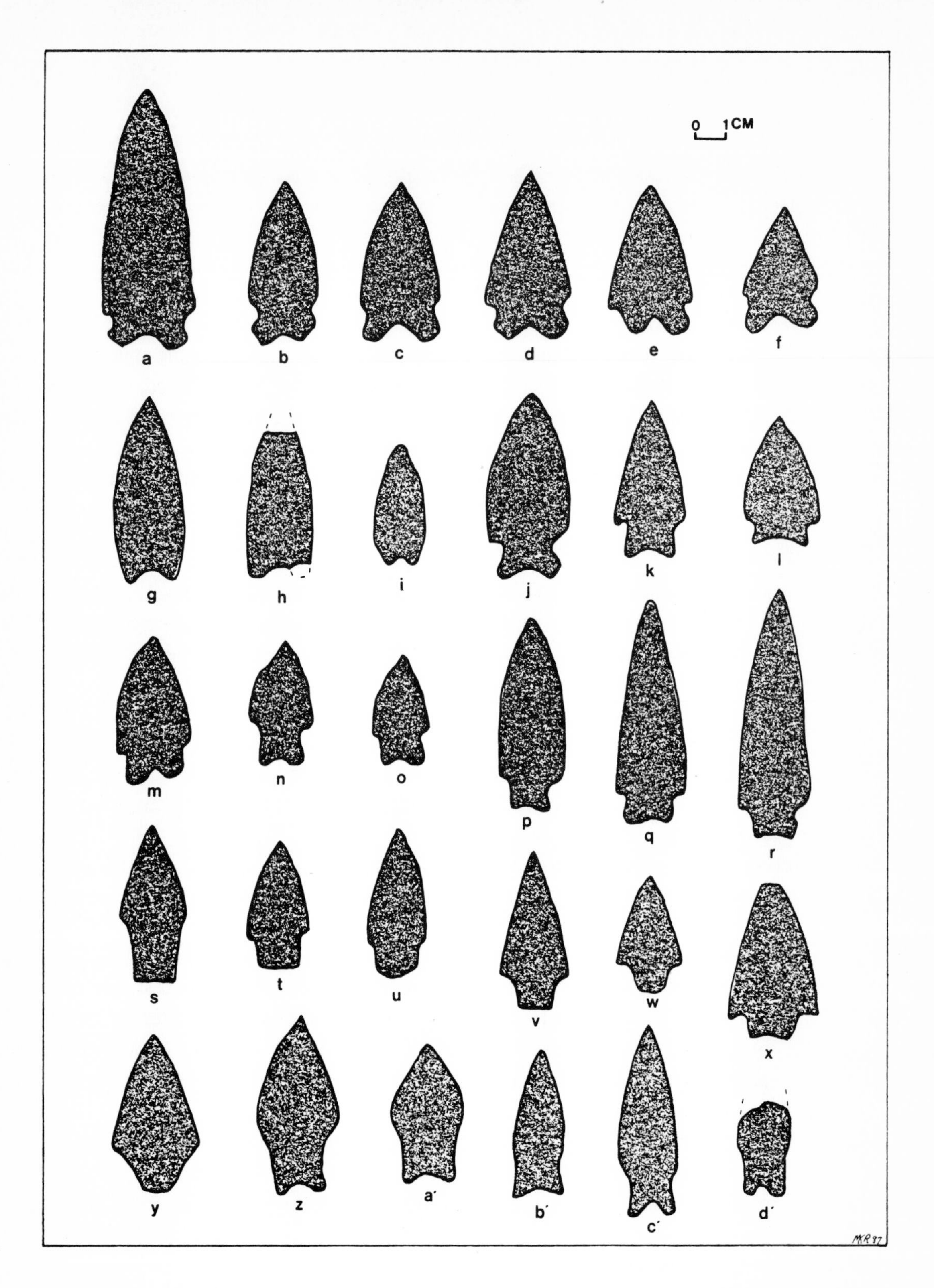

Figure 16. Selected examples of Shuswap horizon projectile point forms. **Type 1**: a–f; **Type 2**: g–i; **Type 3**: j–l; **Type 4**: m–o; **Type 5**: p–r; **Type 6**: s–u; **Type 7**: v–y; **Type 8**: z–d'. Lillooet locality: a,b,j (Stryd 1973a); Lochnore–Nesikep locality: d' (Sanger 1970); Lower Nicola–Spences Bridge locality: z,a',c' (Von Krogh 1978); Nicola Lake locality: b,c,i,s,v (Wyatt 1972); Kamloops locality: e–h,k,m–q,u,x,y (Wilson 1980; Richards and Rousseau 1982); Shuswap Lake: r,t (Sendey 1972); Westside locality: w (Rousseau 1984a); FiSi 19: l (Borden 1952); FgSd 1: b' (Donahue 1975, 1978).

There appears to be a difference in the temporal distribution of the various point types during the Shuswap horizon. Types 1 and 2 do not appear to occur later than about 2800 BP, while types 3, 4, 5 and 8 are found up to ca. 2500 BP. Types 6 and 7 are relatively rare prior to ca. 3000 BP, but after ca. 2800 BP they dominate the assemblages. Future research should clarify and refine the precise temporal ordering of these point types.

Key-shaped formed unifaces/bifaces (Figure 17q,r) are present in Shuswap horizon assemblages and persist until the end of the succeeding Plateau horizon. Fladmark (1978) notes that they appear in Canadian Plateau assemblages after ca. 3300 BP and are absent after ca. 1200 BP. These distinctive items are not present in large numbers, nor are other formed chipped stone tools with the exception of projectile points (Table 7). Formed scrapers are relatively rare, and are usually the small thumbnail endscraper type. Formed scrapers may have been functionally substituted by split cobble tools (Richards and Rousseau 1982:48) and/or by unformed unifacial flakes. The most common chipped stone implements are simple unformed unifacial and bifacial flake tools. Microblades and cores are occasionally found (Sanger 1970:32; Borden 1952:35,36). Ground stone items are rare (Table 8).

Lithic assemblages associated with Shuswap horizon sites display a relative simplicity in composition, workmanship, and technological sophistication compared to later horizons. Locally obtained low to medium quality lithic raw materials such as chert, quartzite, argillite, rhyolite, and especially fine to coarse grained basalts were commonly used. The flaking qualities of these materials may be partly responsible for the stylistically and technologically "crude" appearance of many tools, rather than being indicative of poor lithic technological knowledge or inferior knapping ability. High quality raw materials such as vitreous basalt, chert, chalcedony, and obsidian were also used where locally available.

At the few sites where good preservation prevails, a well-developed bone and antler technology is represented (see Richards and Rousseau 1982:20–75; Wyatt 1972:80–81) (Tables 9 and 10; Figure 17). Notable items include: small, flat, discoidal beads with single circular perforations; bone bracelets(?); bilaterally barbed bone points; harpoon valves; and awls. Bone or antler artifacts with incised decorations are absent.

Artwork, consisting of sculptures and decorated artifacts, is very rare in the Shuswap horizon. A ground and polished zoomorphic pestle with the head of a bear(?) carved on its proximal end was found at EeRb 10, Housepit 9 at Kamloops (Figure 17p), and dates to ca. 3000 BP (Richards and Rousseau 1982:49–51). This is presently the oldest dated example of carved stone artwork found on the Canadian Plateau. An abrader with incised decorations was recovered at EbRc 6 on Nicola Lake and may belong to the Shuswap horizon (Wyatt 1972).

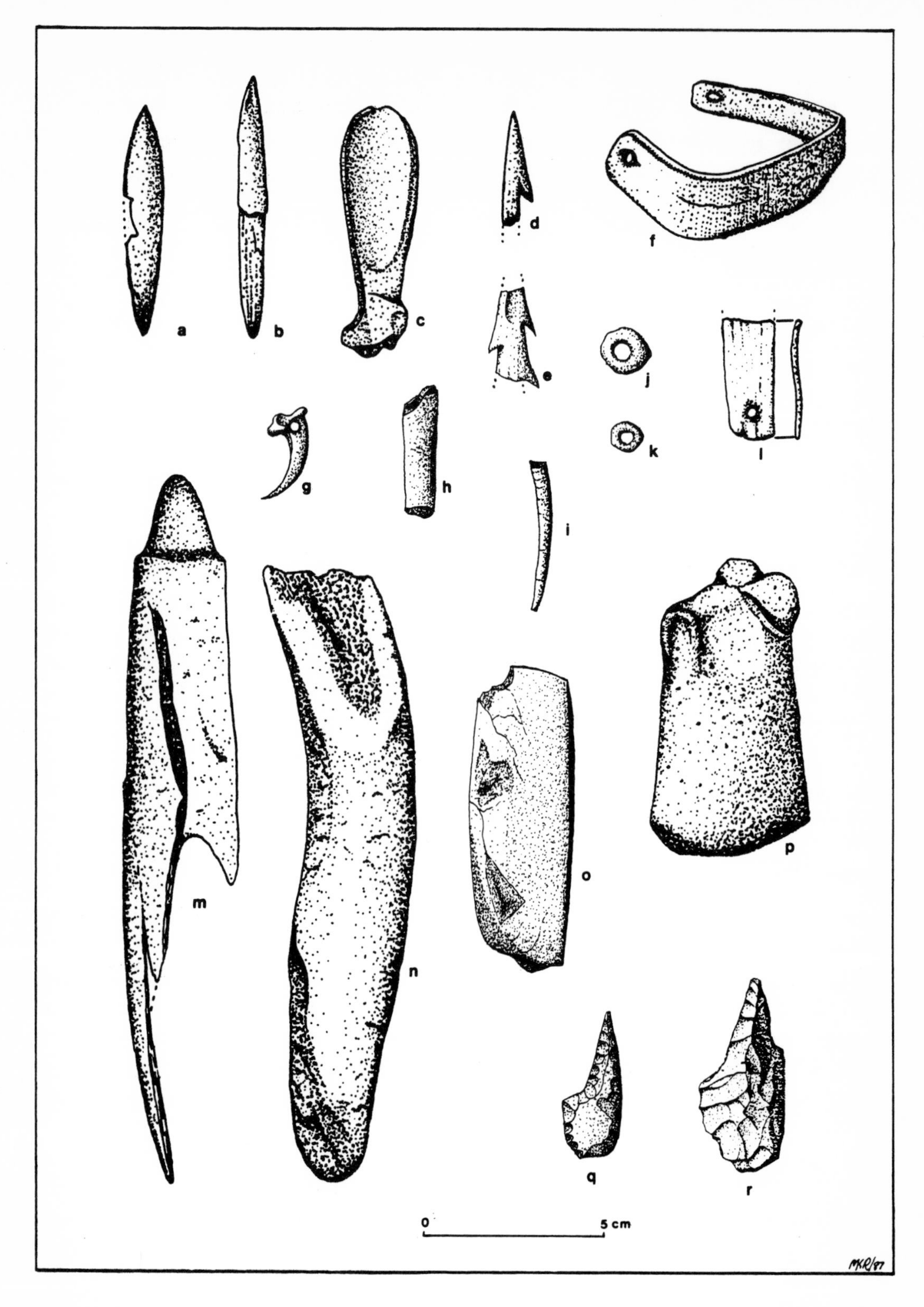

Figure 17. Selected artifacts from Shuswap horizon components. Items **(a,b)**: bone bipoints; **(c)**: bone spoon(?); **(d)**: bone point tip; **(e)**: bilaterally barbed antler point; **(f)**: bone bracelet; **(g)**: perforated eagle claw; **(h)**: sectioned and polished bone bead(?); **(i)**: unmodified Dentalium shell; **(j,k)**: bone disc beads; **(l)**: section of bone bracelet or pendant(?); **(m)**: harpoon valve(?); **(n)**: antler wedge; **(o)**: nephrite celt; **(p)**: top of zoomorphic pestle; **(q,r)**: key-shaped formed unifaces. Artifacts **o** and **r** are from DlQv 39 Rousseau 1984a,b); the rest are from EeRb 10 (Wilson 1980; Richards and Rousseau 1982).

If so, it is the only known item, and these incised decorations are similar to those found on bone and antler implements of the Kamloops horizon.

While excavated burials are rare from this cultural horizon (Table 1), the interment pattern is remarkably similar, considering that the burials are located in widely separated parts of the Canadian Plateau (see Fladmark 1976:28; Mohs 1980a:119; Sanger 1967:28; Sendey 1972:14). The four sites containing burials consist of interments within habitations. Three sites (EdRk 9, EfQu 3, FiRs 1) had flexed burials in pits below the house floor (see Fladmark 1976:28; Sanger 1970:35; Sendey 1972:14). One housepit at EfQu 3 in Shuswap Lake Park contained at least eight individuals (Sendey 1972:14). Burials from all four sites lacked grave inclusions, but red ochre was associated with the interments at Shuswap Lake Park. The burial at EdRk 9 in the Lochnore–Nesikep locality was covered with large boulders (Sanger 1970:35).

Few data are available regarding subsistence, and analysis of faunal remains has not proceeded beyond identification of species (Table 11), skeletal elements, and calculation of minimum number of individuals. Most of the data are from sites EbRc 6 at Nicola Lake and EeRb 10 in Kamloops; both yielded very similar faunal assemblages. Species identified from EbRc 6 include: elk, deer, mountain sheep, black bear, beaver, muskrat, red fox, snowshoe hare, trumpeter swan, fresh water mussels, and unidentified fish (Wyatt 1972:63–66). At EeRb 10, only mammal bones from the 1971 excavations (Wilson 1980) have been identified, and deer, domestic dog, wolf, red fox, striped skunk, porcupine, snowshoe hare and beaver are represented (Galdikas-Brindamour 1972:204). Excavations at this site in 1980 and 1981 secured considerable quantities of faunal remains which have yet to be analyzed in detail, but a preliminary assessment indicates that fresh water mussels, fish (salmon, trout, and other species), birds, and mammals are present (Richards and Rousseau 1982:133). Numerous unidentified fish bones were found in a storage pit within Housepit 13 at site EfQu 3 on the western shores of Shuswap Lake (Sendey 1972:14). In addition, faunal remains from DlQv 39 in the Westside locality of the North Okanagan Valley include elk, yellow-bellied marmot, muskrat, a diving duck, squawfish, trout, and an abundance of freshwater mussel (Rousseau 1984a:115–116; Richards 1983; Kusmer 1984).

These limited data suggest that subsistence during the Shuswap horizon appears to have focused on hunting large and small land mammals and birds, collecting fresh water mussels, and fishing salmon, trout, and other fresh water species. The relative importance of various species is not known, although salmon was undoubtedly an important dietary component. There is presently no evidence for the utilization of plant resources, although it most assuredly took place.

Also important is that Shuswap horizon components have not been recognized in mid-altitude or upland areas. They may exist in these contexts, but the current data suggest that they are probably relatively rare (Pokotylo and Froese 1983; Stryd and Lawhead 1983; Lawhead, Stryd, and Curtin 1986). It is offered that subsistence systems *may* have focused primarily on exploiting resources in valley bottom contexts in close proximity to residential base camps.

Present evidence for inter-regional exchange/interaction is restricted to nephrite artifacts, presumably originating in the Mid-Fraser River region (Fladmark 1982:131). Nephrite artifacts have been found at EbRc 6 on Nicola Lake (Wyatt 1972:80), EeRb 10 in Kamloops (Richards and Rousseau 1982:49), EfQu 3 on Shuswap Lake (Sendey 1972:13), and DlQv 39 on Okanagan Lake (Rousseau 1984b:26). Trade in Northwest Coast shells does not appear to have been significant. An unmodified *Dentalium* shell and a coastal shell of unidentified species with an intentionally serrated edge were recovered from EeRb 10 (Wilson 1980:68; Richards and Rousseau 1982:69).

Extra-Areal Comparisons and Relationships

There are a number of traits shared between the Canadian and Columbia Plateau sub-areas during the period from ca. 4000 to 2400 BP. These include: use of pithouse habitations; exploitation of a wide variety of ungulates (especially deer, elk, and mountain sheep), salmon and other freshwater fish, and fresh water mussels; a subsistence and settlement system which was logistically organized (Binford 1980; Campbell 1985c); well-developed bone and antler industries; and predominant use of the spear and/or atlatl for hunting (Ames and Marshall 1980; Campbell 1985d; Chance and Chance 1977, 1979, 1982; Chatters 1984; Grabert 1968, 1970; Greengo 1986; Jermann 1985; Leonhardy and Rice 1970; Nelson 1969; Schalk and Cleveland 1983; Swanson 1962; Warren 1968). Columbia Plateau pithouse dwellings appear initially around 5000 BP (Ames, Green, and Pfoertner 1981; Sammons-Lohse 1985), which is 1000-1500 years earlier than they are presently known to exist on the Canadian Plateau.

Several Shuswap horizon shouldered and stemmed point forms (i.e., Types 6 and 7 [Figure 16s-y]) have analogues dominating assemblages dated between ca. 4500 and 2500 BP on the Columbia Plateau (Grabert 1968, 1970; Holmes 1966; Jermann 1985; Leonhardy and Rice 1970; Lohse 1985; Nelson 1969; Swanson 1962; Warren 1968). Recognized and defined forms include the "Mahkin Shouldered Lanceolate", "Nespelem Bar", and "Rabbit Island Stemmed" types (see Lohse 1985:346-349).

Shuswap horizon concave-based and eared forms are almost never found on the Columbia Plateau, but they are remarkably similar to Oxbow and

McKean-Hanna-Duncan types found on the Northern Plains. Type 1 has a striking resemblance to the "Oxbow" type, Type 2 with "McKean", and Types 3 and 4 with the "Duncan-Hanna" continuum of forms belonging to the Middle Prehistoric Period on the Northern Plains (Reeves 1969, 1983; Dyck 1983; Wormington and Forbis 1965). Oxbow forms appear at ca. 5000 BP, McKean forms at ca. 4500, and Hanna-Duncan at ca. 3500. Other researchers have also pointed out the similarity between Canadian Plateau and Northern Plains projectile point types (see Sanger 1967:192; 1970:121,122; Wilmeth 1980:2; Donahue 1975:49,53,54); Jermann 1985:25). These types also occur in the southern Canadian Rocky Mountains (Reeves 1974a), and the east Kootenay area of southeastern B.C. (Bussey 1977; Choquette 1984). This amalgam of point styles is roughly contemporaneous over a broad area of northwestern North America and they are classic "horizon markers" (Willey and Phillips 1962:33) indicating some form of interaction between the participant cultures in this style horizon. These styles appear to have diffused westward from the Northern Plains, across the Rocky Mountains and East Kootenays to the Canadian Plateau.

Interaction between the Canadian Plateau and southern Northwest Coast groups is indicated by the presence of coastal trade goods and similarity in some artifact forms. Nephrite was exchanged from the Mid-Fraser River region to the southern coast, and coastal shells such as *Dentalium* were traded inland. Perishable items such as dried salmon or animal skins may have also been a component of coastal-interior exchange.

Several Shuswap horizon point forms are similar to contemporaneous point forms on the southern Northwest Coast. Common in the *Locarno Beach phase* (ca. 3000-2100 BP) are lanceolate chipped stone and ground slate points with parallel stems and narrow shoulders; others have rounded shoulders, concave bases and basal-lateral ears (Borden 1970:Figure 30). In the *Mayne phase* of the Gulf Islands (ca. 5000-3000 BP) chipped stone and ground slate points include contracting stemmed, shouldered and shoulderless forms (Carlson 1970:115-117, Figure 34).

There are also similarities in bone and antler artifact forms, especially presumed fishing implements. A bilaterally barbed antler point or harpoon medial fragment from site EeRb 10 at Kamloops (Wilson 1980:Figure 51d) is similar to harpoons found on the southern coast between ca. 4100 and 3300 BP (McMurdo 1972:112). A harpoon valve, also from EeRb 10 (Richards and Rousseau 1982:55,56, Figure 15d), is similar to those of the Locarno Beach phase (ca. 3000-2100 BP) of the Fraser Delta, in which harpoons are the most common type of fishing implement (Borden 1968:17).

PLATEAU HORIZON

Following the Shuswap horizon is the *Plateau horizon,* estimated to date between ca. 2400 and 1200 BP. The Plateau horizon is represented by numerous excavated components throughout the Canadian Plateau (Table 2; Figure 18). Most components (73%) are from housepit sites, therefore, our conception of Plateau horizon cultural traits and patterns are biased to those represented at this site type.

The commencement of the Plateau horizon at ca. 2400 BP possibly correlates with a significant climatic change that occurred sometime between ca. 3000 to 2000 BP from cool and moist to warmer and drier conditions which were similar to those of today (Figure 14) (Campbell 1985a; Hebda 1982; King 1980; Mack, Rutter, and Valastro 1978; Mathewes 1984). It may be that climatic and environmental changes are at least partially responsible for the shift from the Shuswap horizon to the Plateau horizon.

Horizon Characteristics

Throughout most of the Canadian Plateau, Plateau horizon housepit depressions are generally smaller than those of the preceeding Shuswap horizon and succeeding Kamloops horizon. They average 6.14 m in diameter (s.d. = 1.30), and range between 4.00 and 8.25 m. A notable exception to this pattern is the Mid-Fraser River region where housepits are markedly larger, averaging 9.9 m in diameter (s.d. = 1.72), and range from 8.0 to 11.6 m (see Tables 4 and 5).

Surficially, most Plateau horizon housepit depressions are circular to oval in plan, and lack raised earth rims. In excavated houses, a central hearth feature is usually present, and a few small (.5 - 2.0 m) cooking or storage pits are often found near floor/wall junctures. Housepit walls are usually steep and floors flat, resulting in basin-shaped profiles. Post holes and earth roof insulation zones indicate substantial wooden superstructures covered with earth, similar to the well-known ethnographic model (Boas 1890; Dawson 1891:7; Teit 1900:192-194, 1906:212-215; Laforet and York 1981:118).

Central hearths argue for the presence of a smoke hole at the apex of the roof which may have also functioned as the main house entrance, as there is no present excavated evidence to suggest side entrances. However, a possible interconnecting trench has recently been found between two Plateau horizon housepits at EeRb 70 in the Kamloops locality (Eldridge and Stryd 1983:64). Present along the periphery of many housepit floors are benches which are usually less than one meter wide.

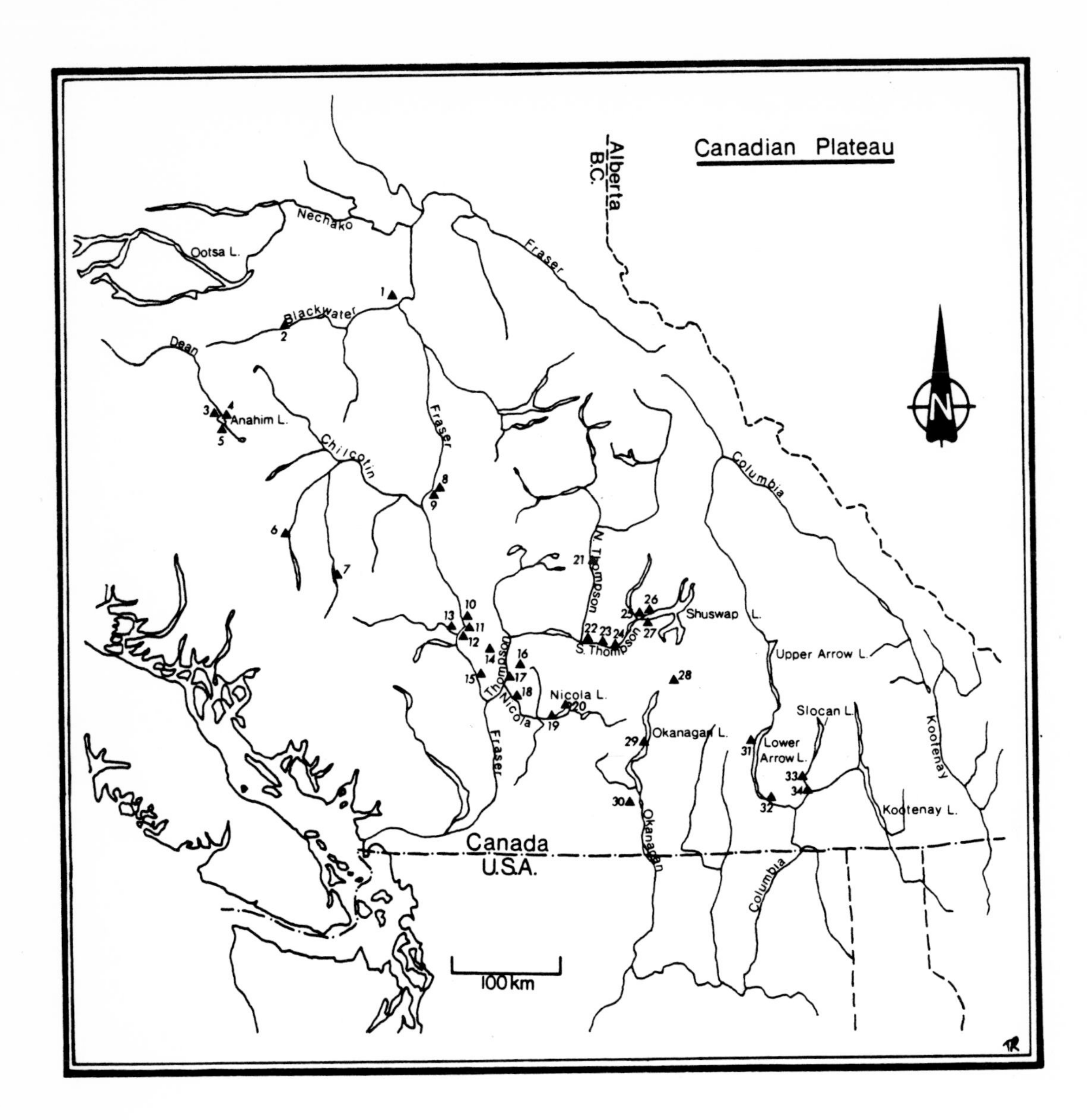

Figure 18. Location of excavated components attributed to the Plateau horizon. Borden site designations and references are listed in Table 2.

Excavations within small circular and oval depressions (2.0 to 4.0 m in diameter) have recovered stone, bone, and antler tools, birch bark sheets and rolls, fire-broken rock, charcoal, fish bones and mammal bones, suggesting these features were used as earth ovens, storage pits, and refuse receptacles (see Carlson 1980:95–96; Wilson 1980:20–21; Richards and Rousseau 1982:96–97,104–107; Von Krogh 1978). Some served single functions, while others were reused for one or more different functions. These features are commonly found in close association with housepits, and sometimes singly or in clusters without housepits.

Projectile points in the Plateau horizon are most always bilaterally barbed with either corner- or basal-notches, and fall into two size groups, one appropriate for tipping spear or atlatl darts, and the other for tipping arrows (Figure 19). The larger points average 4.10 cm in length, 2.60 cm in width, and have a mean neck width of 1.5 cm. The arrow-sized points have a mean length of 2.48 cm, width of 1.73 cm, and neck width of .73 cm (Table 6). The large points are present throughout the Plateau horizon, and the arrow points appear by 1500 BP or possibly as early as 1700 BP. Between ca. 1500 and 1200 BP some assemblages have both sizes, while others have one or the other. Leaf-shaped, lanceolate, corner-notched barbless, and a variety of stemmed point forms also occur, but these usually constitute less than 10% of the points in an assemblage.

Chipped stone endscrapers are much more common than in the preceeding Shuswap horizon, but the most frequent chipped stone tools represented in assemblages continue to be unformed unifacial and bifacial flake implements. Increased use of key-shaped formed uniface/bifaces is apparent compared to the Shuswap horizon. Microblades and cores have been found in several components (Sanger 1970:35,54–69; Wilmeth 1978b:153–157). Ground stone artifacts continue to be rare (Table 8), but may have become somewhat more common after ca. 1900 BP in the Mid-Fraser River region (see below).

There is an observed increase in the quality of chipped stone workmanship during the Plateau horizon compared to the Shuswap horizon. Bifaces and projectile points are often quite large, thin, and symmetrical, and demonstrate well-controlled pressure flaking. The increase in quality of workmanship over the Shuswap horizon may be partly due to an almost exclusive reliance on high quality lithic materials, notably vitreous basalt, as well as cryptocrystalline sillicates and obsidian. Good quality basalts are available from the Baezaeko River area in the north-central interior, as well as from the well-known Arrowstone Hills source near Cache Creek, both of which may originate from the same geological formation (Richards 1987). A variety of good quality cryptocrystalline silicates are obtainable from several sources on the Canadian Plateau, especially from upland Tertiary geological formations in the South Thompson and Thompson River regions (Leaming 1971). Important obsidian sources which were exploited are located near

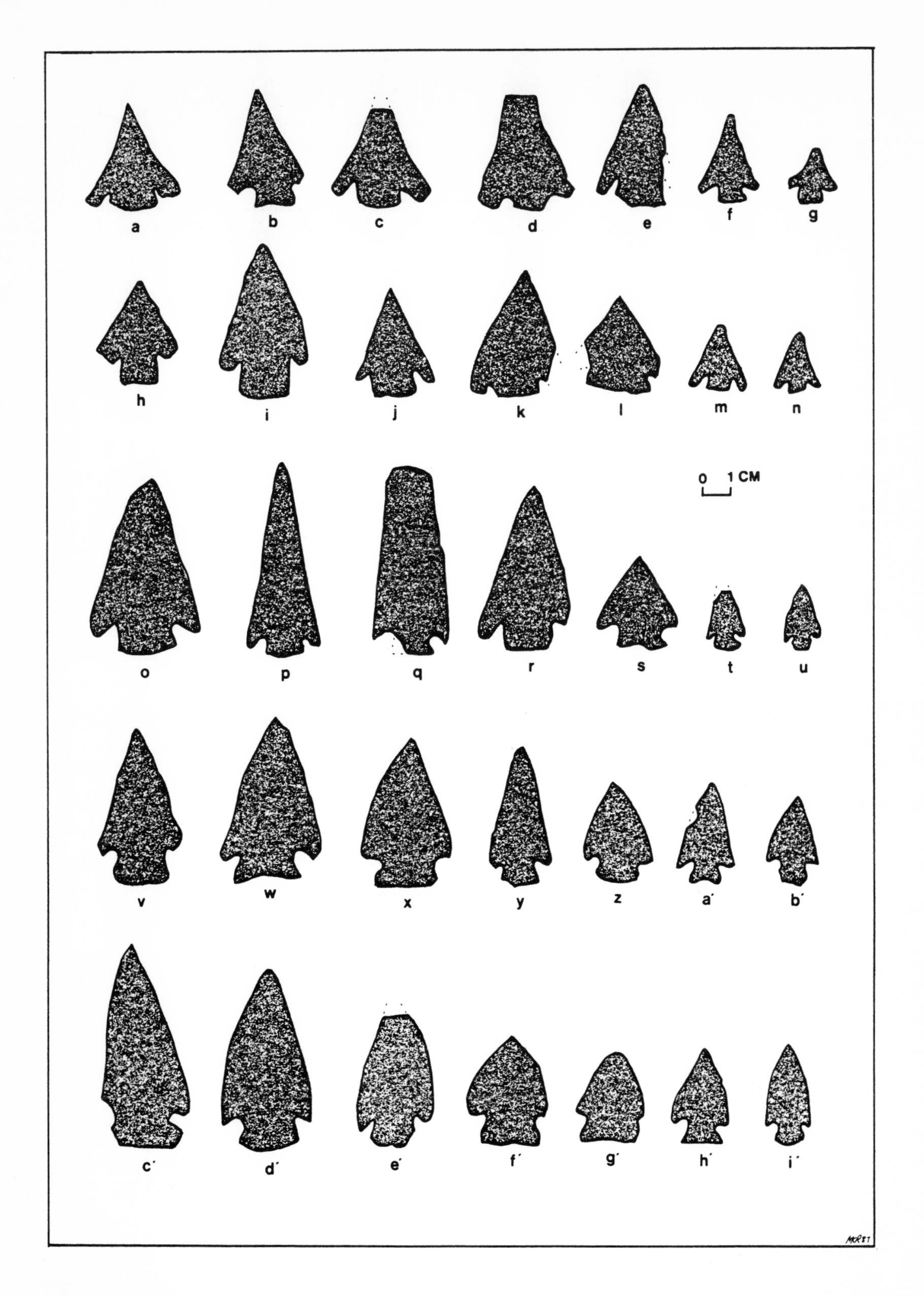

Figure 19. Selected examples of Plateau horizon corner– and basally–notched barbed projectile points. Lillooet locality: a,b,d,f,g,l–n,t,u,a'–d',f'–i' (Stryd 1973a; Richards 1977); Nicola region: c,i (Wyatt 1972); Kamloops locality: j,k,p,r,y (Carlson 1980; Wilson 1980); Arrow Lakes region: e,h,e',q,x (Turnbull 1977; Eldridge 1984).

Anahim Peak in the Chilcotin Region (Nelson and Will 1976), and Mount Edziza near Telegraph Creek in northwestern B.C. (Fladmark 1984, 1985; Godfrey-Smith 1985).

A few components have native copper artifacts, including a rolled cylindrical bead, a pendant, and a triangular knife with a proximal perforation (Von Krogh 1978; Stryd 1973a). Only one component from a housepit site (EeRk 4) is dated, and it belongs to the very end of the horizon (Stryd 1973a:405; Stapp 1984:70). A possible occurrence is suggested by "copper stained" clay in a burial context (Smith 1900:436).

There is an increase in bone, antler, and tooth artifact types over the preceeding Shuswap horizon (Tables 9 and 10), however, we caution that this apparent "elaboration" of perishable industries through time may be illusory and could be related to artifact preservation or sampling. Multiple-barbed unilateral and bilateral bone and antler fixed points or harpoons have been recovered (Figure 20d,e). Tubular beads or gaming pieces made from sections of small mammal or bird longbones have also been found. Composite harpoon valves made of bone appear in the Plateau horizon, and continue to be used during the Kamloops horizon. Perforated mammal tooth pendants or beads appear, as do ground animal incisor tools. There is an increase in both the frequency and variety of coastal shells relative to the Shuswap horizon.

There is some evidence for the use of bark and other organic material for containers. A birch bark container and a partially coiled, imbricated basket have been found (Von Krogh 1978; Richards and Rousseau 1982:96–97). Birch bark may also have been used for lining storage pits and for wrapping stored food. Widespread and common use of birch bark and/or basketry containers probably predates the Plateau horizon, although there is no direct evidence.

It is not yet clear whether portable artwork (i.e., incised objects or sculpture) was common throughout the Canadian Plateau during the Plateau horizon. In the Mid-Fraser River region, bone, antler, and steatite artifacts with incised decorations have been recovered at EeRk 4 from Housepit 21 (ca. 1500 BP) and Housepit 22, Component 2 (ca. 1900 BP) (Stryd 1973a). Additional components containing similar decorated items that *may* belong to the Plateau horizon include: Housepits 6, 8, 11, 19 and 23 at EeRk 4; Housepit 1 at EeRl 22; Housepit 1 at EeRk 7; and *Zone 1* at EdRk 7 (see Stryd 1972, 1973a, 1980, 1983b; Sanger 1970). We are somewhat reticent about accepting the latter components because of possible mixing with later Kamloops horizon components which are also present in each housepit. In the Kamloops locality, a digging stick handle (Figure 20a) and a bone object (Figure 20c) attributable to the initial half of the Plateau horizon are decorated with incised parallel lines (Carlson 1980:114;

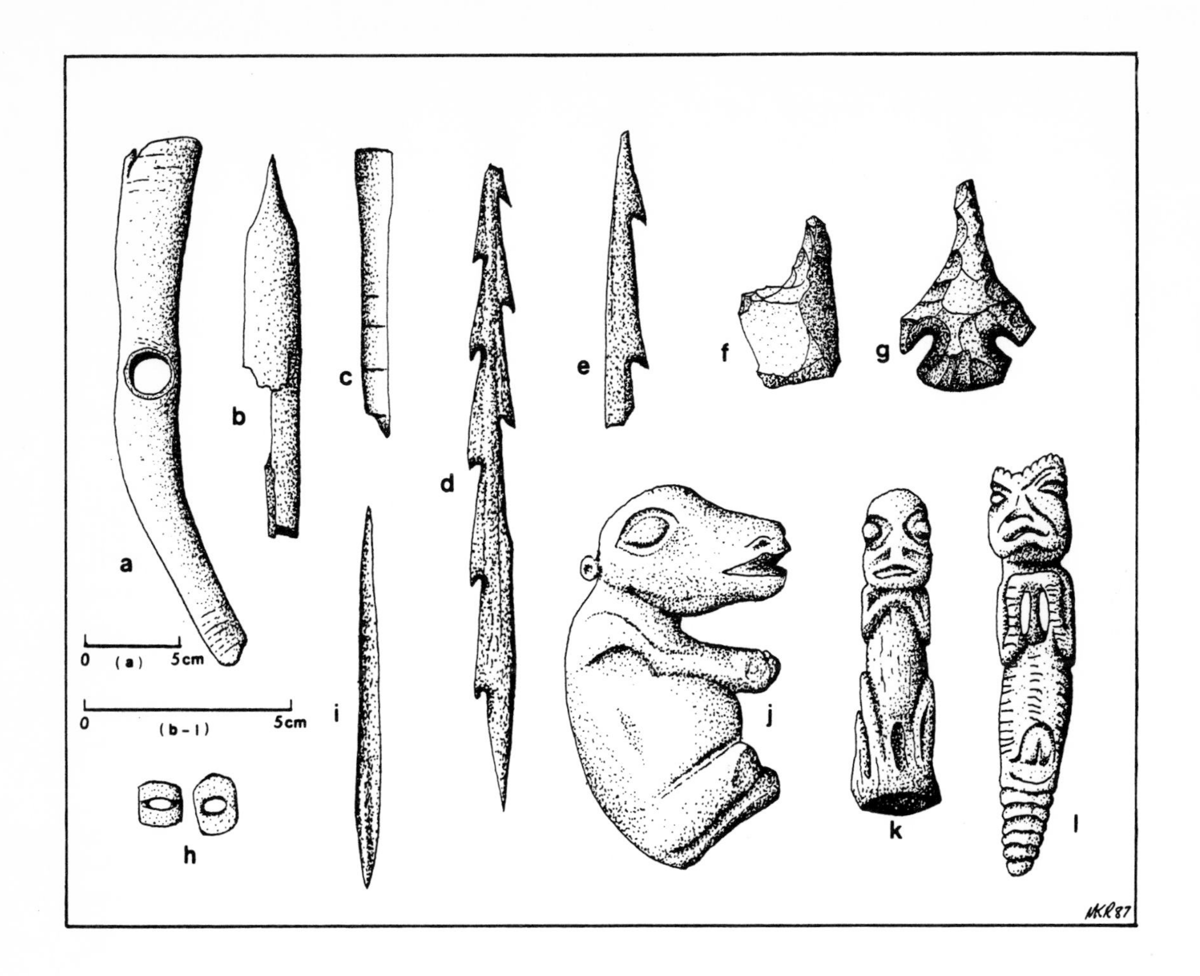

Figure 20. Selected artifacts from Plateau horizon components. Item **(a)**: decorated digging stick handle [EeRc 44] Eldridge and Stryd 1983); **(b)**: bone awl [EdRa 22]; **(c)**: incised bone tube [EeRa 4] (Carlson 1980); **(d)**: bilaterally barbed point; **(e)**: unilaterally barbed point [EeRb 70] (Eldridge and Stryd 1983); **(f)**: key-shaped formed uniface; **(g)**: drill recycled from projectile point [EeRb 3] (Wilson 1980); **(h)**: oblong beads [EdRa 22] (Carlson 1980); **(i)**: bone bipoint [EeRb 70] (Eldridge and Stryd 1983); **(j)**: zoomorphic (bear?) stone sculpture; **(k,l)**: antler figurines [EeRk 4] (Stryd 1973a, 1981b). Figures **j–l** may belong to the early Kamloops horizon.

Eldridge and Stryd 1983:180). In summary, it appears that incised objects, sculptures, and ground stone tools such as nephrite celts, hand mauls, steatite and slate artifacts were rare throughout most of the Canadian Plateau during the Plateau horizon, however, they may have become more common by ca. 1900 BP, especially in the Mid-Fraser River region.

Few burials are attributable to the Plateau horizon, and a great deal remains to be learned about burial modes during this period. In two instances a few scattered, charred human bones have been found in non-housepit hearths or concentrations of charcoal (Mohs 1982:109; Fladmark 1976:28). These may not be primary interments, but rather cremation loci. Four partially cremated child interments were found near Kamloops (Smith 1900:436), each burial was associated with a large number of grave goods, including artifacts not commonly found in other types of sites (e.g., nephrite celts, digging stick handles, net sinkers, and ***Dentalium*** beads). At the Fountain site (EeRl 19) in the Lillooet locality, an adult female interred in a semi-flexed position within a shallow, oval, birch bark-lined pit was dated to ca. 1400 BP, placing the burial near the very end of the Plateau horizon (McLeod and Skinner 1987). At EeRh 1 near Cache Creek in the Thompson River region, a wooden cist burial marked by a boulder cairn containing the remains of an infant (Burial 8a) excavated by Borden in the mid-1950s recently provided a radiocarbon age determination of 1960±400 BP (SFU 292) on bone collagen. However, there is doubt expressed about the validity of this date due to the small amount of carbon assayed (Pokotylo, Binkley, and Curtin 1987:8). It is likely that this burial actually dates to the initial half of the Kamloops horizon, as other associated and similarly disposed burials from the site produced dates between 1300 and 700 BP.

An infant burial recovered from a pit extending below the floor of Housepit 19 at site EeRk 4 in the Lillooet locality was associated with an unusual assortment of grave goods. These included a zoomorphic ornamental comb, a rattlesnake-woman figurine (Figure 20l), a siltstone bear(?) figurine (Figure 20j), an anthropomorphic face pendant, and 246 ***Dentalium*** beads (Stryd 1973a:425-427, 1981b). Stryd (1973a, 1981b) initially attributed the burial to the "early Kamloops phase" (ca. 1400-1000 BP), however, he has recently suggested that it should be reassigned to the Shuswap horizon (Lawhead, Stryd, and Curtin 1986:29). Housepit 19 was completely excavated and the floor yielded Plateau and Kamloops horizon projectile points and radiocarbon dates which range between ca. 1500 and 1250 BP (Stryd 1973a, 1980:14). Two anthropomorphic figurines (Figure 20k) and a figurine preform were also found on the house floor. Some of the burial inclusions have incised decorations (Stryd 1981a:9, 10). Incised decorations are known to be limited to Plateau and Kamloops horizon bone and antler artifacts, and are absent during the Shuswap horizon. Similar anthropomorphic carvings were found in Housepits 5 and 23 at EeRk 4 which have yielded dates of ca. 1400-1550 BP (Stryd 1980:14).

In summary, we suggest that the Housepit 19 burial and associated artwork may be attributable to the late Plateau horizon, or possibly the early Kamloops horizon. A radiocarbon assay of the burial would help to resolve this problem.

There is a paucity of available data on subsistence for the Plateau horizon (Table 11). The most significant observed change over the preceeding Shuswap horizon is the commencement of intensive exploitation of mid-altitude root resources (see Pokotylo and Froese 1983), although how widespead a phenomenon this practice was is difficult to assess with the present limited data. The earliest known antler digging stick handle (Figure 20a) was recovered from site EeRc 44 near Kamloops which dates to ca. 2400 BP (Eldridge and Stryd 1983:59). In the 19th Century, similar antler handles were part of a composite root digging tool (Teit 1900:231; 1909:514).

Stable-carbon isotope ($\delta^{13}C$) analysis of human skeletons dated radiometrically between ca. 1600 and 1200 BP in the Lillooet locality suggest that on average, approximately 60% of the dietary protein had a marine origin (salmon and steelhead trout); a lesser value of around 40% was determined from a single individual from the Kamloops locality; and about 40% is also suggested for two individuals at the confluence of the Columbia and Kootenay Rivers (Chisholm 1986). These are similar to the values obtained for the ensuing Kamloops horizon.

Trade among Canadian Plateau groups was intensified relative to the Shuswap horizon. Exchange of nephrite coastal shells, and possibly high quality lithic raw materials increased. Coastal shells were obtained from Northwest Coast groups, probably via the Mid-Fraser River region.

Extra-Areal Comparisons and Relationships

Nephrite trade with southern Northwest Coast groups was greatly intensified during the Plateau horizon. Nephrite celts are common in Marpole phase (ca. 2350–1500 BP) components, but rare in the preceding Locarno Beach phase (ca. 3000–2100 BP) (Borden 1970; Burley 1980). Increased exchange, and thus interaction, with Northwest Coast cultures after the onset of the Marpole phase may partly explain why the Mid-Fraser River region deviates somewhat from the rest of the Canadian Plateau during the Plateau horizon (see Hayden *et al* 1985).

During the period between ca. 3300 and 1500 BP there is evidence for a trans-Rocky Mountain exchange network involving Plateau, East Kootenay, Rocky Mountain, and Northern Plains cultures. Northwest Coast *Olivella* and *Dentalium* shells, Canadian Plateau nephrite, Kootenay argillite and Top of the World chert (from the East Kootenays) were exchanged (Choquette 1981:27,33; Forbis 1960; Neuman 1975; Reeves 1974b:23,24,40; 1983:80,81,87,93,94,97,98; Brumley 1980:84,85;

Quigg 1981:64,65; Gryba 1980; Richards 1984). Items of Northern Plains origin have not been found on the Canadian Plateau to indicate what was being traded westward, although perishables such as buffalo robes may have been involved, as recorded for the ethnographic Shuswap and Thompson (Teit 1900:259, 1909:536).

There are many similarities between the Columbia and Canadian Plateaus during the period from ca. 2400 to 1200 BP. These include: use of winter pithouses; heavy reliance on salmon; exploitation of deer, root resources, and fresh water mussels; a logistically organized subsistence and settlement system (Binford 1980; Campbell 1985c); use of storage pits; and predominant use of the spear and/or atlatl for hunting (Campbell 1985d; Chance and Chance 1977, 1979, 1982; Chatters 1984; Grabert 1968, 1970; Greengo 1986; Jermann 1985; Leonhardy and Rice 1970; Schalk and Cleveland 1983; Swanson 1962; Nelson 1969; Warren 1968).

Large basally-notched, barbed points appear in assemblages on the Columbia Plateau by ca. 2700–2500 BP (see Grabert 1968, 1970; Greengo 1982, 1986; Holmes 1966; Leonhardy and Rice 1970; Lohse 1985; Nelson 1969; Warren 1968). Large basally-notched points do not appear until after ca. 2400 BP on the Canadian Plateau, suggesting perhaps, that this point style originated on the Columbia Plateau and was adopted by Canadian Plateau groups at least one or two centuries later. Large corner-notched barbed point forms first appear around ca. 3000 BP on the Columbia Plateau (Greengo 1982; Lohse 1985; Nelson 1969; Rice 1972) which is at least 600 years earlier than they are known to appear on the Canadian Plateau.

Medium to large corner-notched points with convex bases and small barbs found in Plateau horizon components are very similar in style to Pelican Lake corner-notched points found on the Northern Plains (Dyck 1983; Wormington and Forbis 1965; Reeves 1983) (Figures 16, 18). The *Pelican Lake phase* began as early as approximately 3300 BP on the Northern Plains, and terminated between ca. 1850 and 1750 BP (Dyck 1983:105; Reeves 1983:5). Reeves observes that it terminates earliest in the middle Missouri area and at progressively later dates to the west. It appears, then, that this point style originated far to the east and spread westward across the Plains, the Rocky Mountains (Reeves 1974a) and East Kootenays (Bussey 1977; Choquette 1984), to the Columbia Plateau, Canadian Plateau, and southern Northwest Coast. The approximate coeval distribution of this barbed corner-notched projectile point type over such a large area of Northwestern North America may have been facilitated by extensive culture group interaction brought about by a high degree of mobility, trade ties, or perhaps by diffusion of an innovation relating to a more efficient hunting weapon system.

There are many instances of material culture similarities between Plateau horizon assemblages and contemporaneous southern coastal asssemblages. The *Skamel phase* (ca. 2300–1750 BP) of the Yale locality includes barbed, corner-notched chipped stone points, a variety of small specialized formed tools, and cryptocrystalline lithic materials not used in previous phases (Borden 1968:16; Archer 1980:38). Present in the Marpole phase of the Fraser Delta locality and the Marpole culture type of the Gulf of Georgia region are corner and basally-notched, barbed, chipped stone points (Borden 1968, 1970; Mitchell 1971; Burley 1980). Corner and basally-notched, barbed points similar to those of Marpole, but smaller in size are found in the *Whalen II phase* (ca. 1600–1150 BP) of the Fraser Delta (Borden 1968, 1970).

KAMLOOPS HORIZON

The *Kamloops horizon* is the last prehistoric cultural horizon to occur on the Canadian Plateau. The Kamloops horizon is estimated to date between ca. 1200 and 200 BP, and is essentially an expanded integrative unit partially derived and modelled from the "Kamloops phase" as originally defined by Sanger (1968a). There are more excavated components of this horizon than for either of the preceding ones (Table 3; Figure 21), and the majority of these (69%) are from housepit sites. Climate and environmental conditions during the Kamloops horizon appear to have approximated those of today (Figure 14) (Hansen 1955; Mack, Rutter, and Valastro 1978; King 1980; Hebda 1982; Campbell 1985a).

We disagree with previous applications of the term "Kamloops phase" to describe and refer to late prehistoric manifestations represented in distinctively different archaeological regions on the Canadian Plateau which date between ca. 1200 to 200 years BP (e.g., see Sanger 1968a, 1970; Stryd 1973a,b; Pokotylo and Froese 1983; Pokotylo, Binkley, and Curtin 1987; Matson, Ham, and Bunyan 1981; Magne and Matson 1984). We argue that the label "Kamloops *horizon*" is more appropriate because a cultural horizon is essentially an *integrative* construct which recognizes a general level of inter-regional cultural similarity, while at the same time acknowledging that certain regional differences exist. The Kamloops phase is a *descriptive* archaeological unit that should henceforth be recognized as existing *only* within the South Thompson River-Western Shuswap Lakes region where it has been defined by Wilson (1980), and more recently by Rousseau and Richards (1985).

Horizon Characteristics

Excavated Kamloops horizon housepits are highly variable in size. They average 8.66 m in diameter (s.d. = 2.32 m), and range between 5.0 and 12.0 m (see Table 4). Our field observation of unexcavated probable Kamloops horizon housepits suggests that they range up to 20 m in diameter, and therefore the

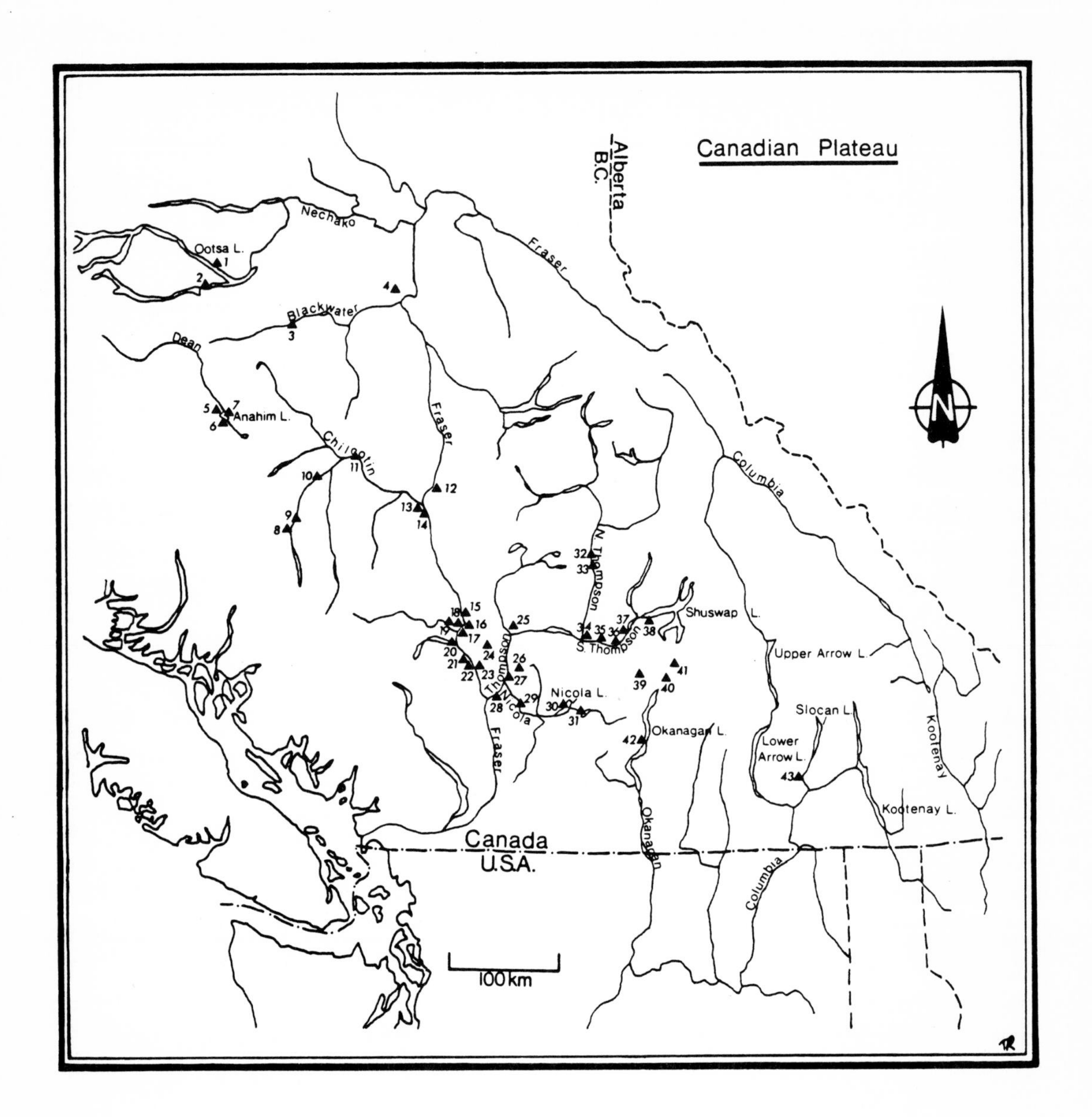

Figure 21. Location of excavated components attributed to the Kamloops horizon. Borden site designations and references are presented in Table 3.

mean diameter derived from the excavated sample may be low. They are oval, circular, rectangular, or square in plan, and usually have prominent raised earth rims. In many instances, side entrances are visible, especially on rectilinear housepits. The remains of passageways between housepits are present at one site in the South Thompson River–Western Shuswap Lakes region (see Mohs 1981:Figure 6.2).

Excavations indicate that roof insulation deposits are usually very thin or absent, especially in rectilinear housepits, suggesting light pole and mat structures as in Boas' (1890:635) ethnographic description of an alternative form of winter habitation to the "classic" pithouse (Dawson 1891:7; Teit 1900:192–194). The paucity of substantial post holes in excavated rectilinear housepits further suggests light roof structures. Circular and oval housepits are more similar to ethnographically described pithouses which have substantial wooden superstructures covered with earth for insulation (Dawson 1891:7; Teit 1900:192–195, 1906:213; Laforet and York 1981:115–121). Central hearths are found in most housepits, and small (.5 - 2.0 m dia.) cooking or storage pits are often found within the houses at or near floor/wall junctures.

Several small, circular or oval external depressions which functioned as food storage pits, or occasionally as earth ovens are often associated with Kamloops horizon housepits. These small depressions average about 2.0 m in diameter, and range from between 1.0 to 3.5 m. Sites containing only storage pits are common near salmon fisheries on rivers and lakes, and these are believed to date to the Kamloops and possibly Plateau horizons.

Ubiquitous in Kamloops horizon assemblages is the *"Kamloops side-notched point"* originally defined by Stryd (1972:20). It is a small triangular arrow point having a mean maximum length of 2.04 cm, width of 1.32 cm, and an average neck width of .72 cm (Table 6). Most have small, narrow, opposing side notches, and straight to slightly convex or concave basal margins (Figure 22). Occasionally, points of identical style, but larger size are found which may have been used to tip spears or atlatl darts (Figure 22 o'–r') (see Sanger 1970:Figure 21s,t; Wilmeth 1978b:Plate XII; Wilson 1980:Figure 39h; Richards 1982:Figure 14; Eldridge and Stryd 1983:Figure 49). These larger side-notched points almost always have straight basal margins, and appear to be temporally restricted to the very end of the horizon.

A more rare variant form is the *"Kamloops multi-notched point"*, believed to date between ca. 400 and 100 BP (see Richards 1977). It differs from the Kamloops side-notched point in that there are additional notches (up to 4) along one lateral blade margin (Figure 22y–b'), and it is slightly larger, having an average maximum length of 2.94 cm, width of 1.68 cm, and mean neck width of

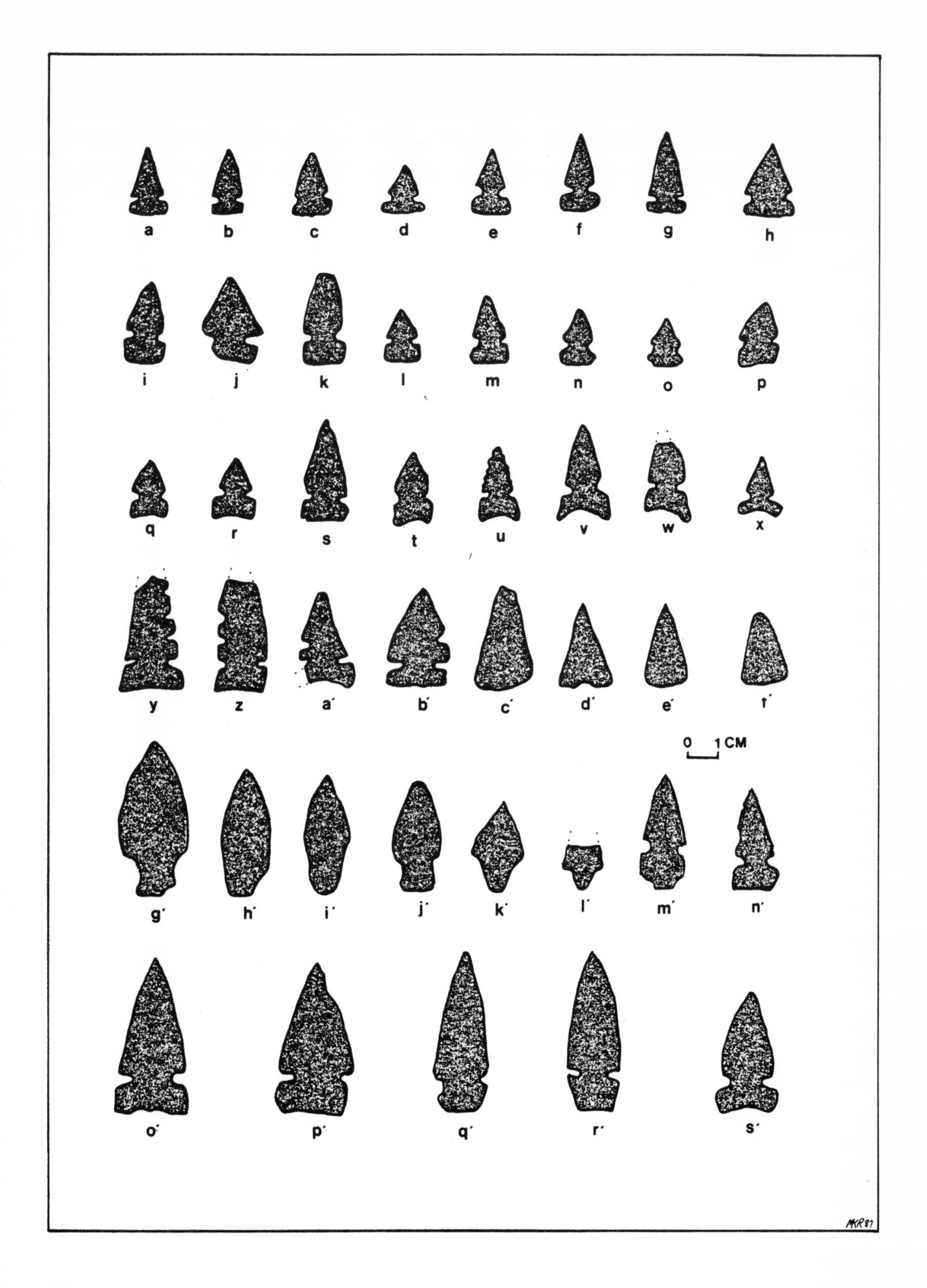

Figure 22. Selected examples of Kamloops horizon projectile points. Lillooet locality: a,b,d,e,x,y,z,a',c',d',e',h',l' (Stryd 1973a; Richards 1977); Tezli Lake: c,p,s (Donahue 1975); Vallican: f,g,h,o,r,t–v (Eldridge 1984); Kamloops locality: i–l,q,w,p',q' (Wilson 1980); Anahim Lake locality: m,n,b',g',i'–k',o' (Wilmeth 1978b); Eagle Lake locality: m',n' Magne and Matson 1984); Lochnore–Nesikep locality: r' (Sanger 1970).

.89 cm (Table 6). Multi-notched Kamloops points have not been observed in any excavated components on the Columbia Plateau, North Okanagan Valley, or Arrow Lakes region, although it can be argued that the sample of excavated assemblages from the latter two regions is too small to ascertain their absence. However, it may be that they are unique to ethnographic Chilcotin, Thompson, and Shuswap territories.

In the Chilcotin region, a point form similar to the "Kavik" and "Klo-kut" types from Alaska and the Yukon (Campbell 1968; Morlan 1973) is found in association with Kamloops side-notched points within territory ethnographically occupied by the Athapaskan Carrier and Chilcotin. These small contracting stem arrow points are considered to indicate Athapaskan cultural affiliation (Wilmeth 1978b), and it has been noted that they are more common in northern Chilcotin region assemblages (Matson *et al* 1980:184).

Biface technology in the Kamloops horizon is similar to that of the Plateau horizon. Fine pressure-finishing of points and knives was common, however, there is variation in the quality of retouch and some rather poorly-made specimens are present. Most formed tools are well made, and a slight reduction in size compared to those of the preceding Plateau horizon is observed. "Pentagonal" formed bifaces are common during this horizon (Figure 23h,i). At present there is no firm evidence to suggest that microblade technology was used during the Kamloops horizon.

An increase in the quality, quantity, and variety of ground stone artifacts made of slate, nephrite, and steatite is evident during the Kamloops horizon (Table 8; Figure 23). Steatite was often carved into zoomorphic or anthropomorphic forms which exhibit a high degree of workmanship and creativity (Sanger 1968a; Stryd 1983b). Use of native copper to fashion decorative artifacts continued.

There is evidence for the continued use of bark artifacts. Birch bark containers are found, including stitched examples (Sanger 1968a:140, 1970:Figures 7, 10; Stryd 1972:22). Birch bark was also used for lining storage pits as it was in the ethnographic period (Dawson 1890:9). A plaited sagebrush bark mat has also been found (Stryd 1972:22). Undoubtedly, woven basketry containers were also used, as they were present in the preceding Plateau horizon, and were very important to historic Interior Salish groups (see Teit 1900:187-191, 1906:205-207; 1909:487-491).

There is an increase in the variety and frequency of bone, antler, and tooth artifacts in relation to the Plateau horizon (Tables 9 and 10). Incised decorations on bone and antler artifacts are common in the Kamloops horizon,

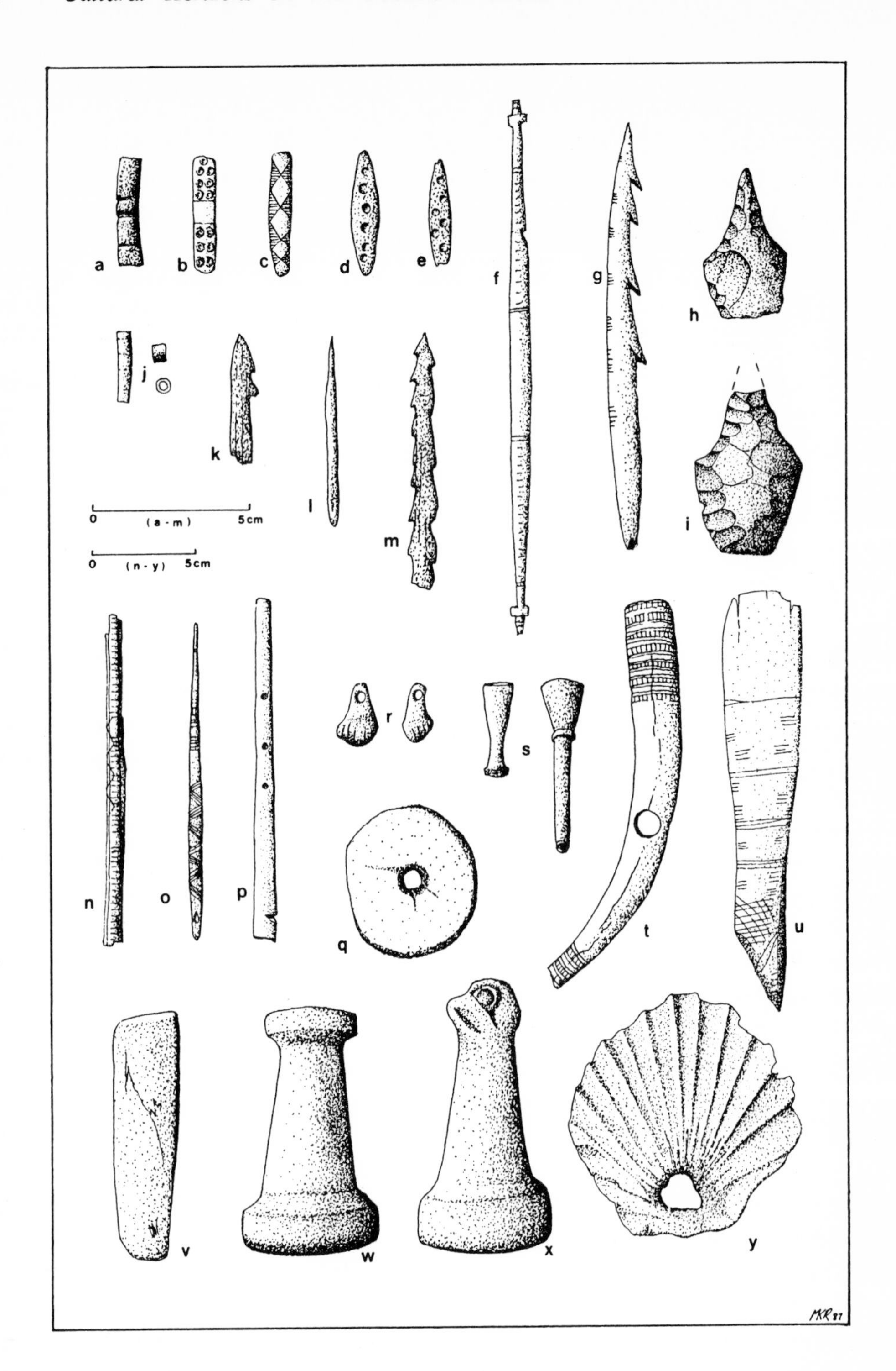

Figure 23. Selected artifacts from Kamloops horizon components. Item **(a)**: polished and incised bone bead or gaming piece [EeRc 44] (Eldridge and Stryd 1983); **(b–e)**: bone gaming pieces (b:EcRh 11 [Von Krogh 1978]; c: EdRk 3 [Sanger 1970]; d,e: EeRc 44 [Eldridge and Stryd 1983]); **(f)**: miniature bone bow; (g): decorated unilaterally barbed antler point/harpoon [EeQw 1] (Sanger 1968a); **(h,i)**: pentagonal bifaces h: EdRk 5 [Sanger 1970]; i: EeRk 4 [Stryd 1973a]); **(j)**: *Dentalium* beads [EeRh 1] (Pokotylo, Binkley, and Curtin 1987); **(k)**: unilaterally barbed point; **(l)**: bone needle; **(m)**: bilaterally barbed point [EeRc 44] (Eldridge and Stryd 1983); **(n)**: decorated bone drinking tube (?) [EeRh 1] (Pokotylo, Binkley, and Curtin 1987); **(o)**: decorated bone needle [EbRi 7] (Skinner and Copp 1986); **(p)**: bone whistle; **(q)**: spindle whorl [EdRk 3] (Sanger 1970); **(r)**: perforated elk teeth [EeRh 1] (Pokotylo, Binkley, and Curtin 1987); **(s)**: steatite trumpet pipes (left: EdRk 3 [Sanger 1970], right: EeQw 1 [Sanger 1968a]); **(t)**: decorated digging stick handle; **(u)**: decorated bone sap scraper; **(v)**: nephrite celt [EeQw 1] (Sanger 1968a); **(w,x)**: hand mauls [EdRk 8]; **(y)**: perforated *Pectin* shell [EdRk 3] (Sanger 1970).

and consist of geometric patterns of parallel lines, ticks, and "circles and dots" (Figure 23) (see also Stryd 1973b:179). They are more commonly found on bone artifacts than antler. ***Dentalium*** shell beads were also sometimes decorated (Smith 1900:431).

Burial practices in the Kamloops horizon are reasonably well documented. The dominant pattern is the primary flexed interment in an unmarked shallow pit. Other types of burials include wooden cist inhumations marked with rock cairns, multiple tomb burials, and talus slope burials (see Smith 1900:434–440; Sanger 1968a:140–143, 1968c). Excavated burials indicate that body orientation is commonly east–west or west–east, and some had fires built over the graves (see Dawson 1891:13; Skinner and Copp 1986; Pokotylo, Binkley, and Curtin 1987). Some are associated with birch bark sheeting, tule matting and cordage, suggesting that body wrapping and binding may have been a common practice.

In addition to faunal remains and common utilitarian implements (i.e., projectile points, bifaces, flake tools, bark containers), Kamloops horizon burials are also occasionally associated with "primitive valuables" (Dalton 1975), which include nephrite celts, steatite sculptures, copper ornaments, decorated bone and antler artifacts (e.g., digging stick handles, drinking tubes, gaming pieces), perforated elk teeth, shells or shell beads of coastal origin, and red and yellow ochre (Figure 23) (see also Sanger 1968a; Skinner and Copp 1986; Pokotylo, Binkley, and Curtin 1987). Many of these items are made of imported raw materials, for which considerable investments of time and energy were involved in their acquisition or manufacture. Their differential occurrence in Kamloops horizon burials has been interpreted as being indicative of variability in individual wealth and/or social status (see Hayden *et al* 1985:190; Pokotylo, Binkley, and Curtin 1987).

As with the preceding horizons, few specific details are available regarding subsistence practices (Table 11). Stable–carbon isotope analysis ($\delta^{13}C$) indicates that marine protein (salmon and steelhead trout) constituted between 40 to 60% of the dietary protein of the people living on the Canadian Plateau during the Kamloops horizon (Chisholm and Nelson 1983:85; Lovell 1982:Table 1; Lovell *et al* 1983; Chisholm 1986:115–124). Recent research by Chisholm (1986) has indicated that during the Kamloops horizon, the average percentage of marine protein in the aboriginal diet decreases slightly with increased distance up the Fraser and Thompson drainages. Individuals living in the Lillooet locality consumed an average of 60% marine protein; while the values are 56% for the Thompson River region, 48% for the South Thompson River, and 41% for the Adams River. Data for the North Okanagan Valley indicate a south to north decline in reliance on salmon. One individual from Penticton indicates 57% marine protein, one from Peachland 44%, and three from Kelowna were averaged at only 19%. In the Arrow Lakes region, salmon reliance also decreases with increased distance upstream. A greater degree of variation is noted near the confluence of the Columbia and Kootenay Rivers, a pattern which is attributed to higher population mobility resulting from long-distance travelling to choice fishing stations (e.g., Kettle Falls) (Chisholm 1986:121).

A sophisticated fishing technology is indicated at many sites by the presence of bone and antler leisters, unilaterally and bilaterally barbed points and harpoons (Figure 23), composite toggling harpoons, possible fish hook barbs, and small bipoints resembling those used by the ethnographic Shuswap and Thompson (Teit 1900:251-253, 1909:525).

There was a continued reliance on wild root resources, evidenced by dated root-roasting ovens (Pokotylo and Froese 1983), and the occurrence of antler digging stick handles (Sanger 1968a). One significant difference in hunting technology apparent in this horizon is the almost complete dependence on the bow and arrow, as reflected by the preponderance of small arrow-sized points.

Inter-regional trade appears to have been significant during this horizon. Important non-perishable commodities include vitreous basalt, nephrite celts, ground slate items, steatite carvings, whalebone, and coastal shells.

Extra-Areal Comparisons and Relationships

Several general similarities are apparent between the Canadian and Columbia Plateaus from ca. 1200 to 200 BP. Both sub-areas are characterized by: use of winter pithouses; a heavy reliance on salmon, deer, and root resources; continued hunting of large ungulates (e.g., mountain sheep and elk), a marked decrease in exploitation of fresh water mussels compared to earlier periods; a logistically organized subsistence and settlement system (Binford 1980); use of food storage pits; well-developed chipped stone, ground stone, bone and antler industries; and predominant use of the bow and arrow for hunting (Campbell 1985d; Chance and Chance 1977, 1979, 1982; Grabert 1968; Greengo 1986; Holmes 1966; Jermann 1985; Leonhardy and Rice 1970; Nelson 1969; Swanson 1962; Warren 1968).

Similarities in projectile point styles are also evident. At the begining of the Kamloops horizon (ca. 1200-1100 BP) small, corner- or basal-notched, barbed points so common on the Columbia Plateau are occasionally present in small numbers in assemblages on the Canadian Plateau. In most regions on the Columbia Plateau, small side-notched points appear to be absent before ca. 1000 BP (Chance and Chance 1977, 1979, 1982; Grabert 1968, 1970; Holmes 1966; Jermann 1985; Leonhardy and Rice 1970; Nelson 1969; Warren 1968). Only on the northern Columbia Plateau, from ca. 1000-600 BP to the contact period, do small side-notched points predominate in numbers over the corner- or basal-notched, barbed types. In very late prehistoric to early contact sites (ca. 600–150 BP) throughout the southern and central Columbia Plateau, small side-notched points are occasionally found (Holmes 1966; Nelson 1969; Leonhardy and Rice 1970). This probably reflects interaction with Plains rather than Canadian Plateau groups.

On the Northern Plains, small side-notched points referred to as the Avonlea type appear around 1750 BP (Reeves 1983:16; Dyck 1983:122; Vickers 1986:90). Their appearance is thought to mark the initial use of the bow and arrow. Points of this style, with a few exceptions, are absent from the Canadian Plateau. "Plains" and "Prairie side-notched" types predominate after ca. 1400 BP (Wormington and Forbis 1965; Dyck 1983; Reeves 1983; Vickers 1986:95). The data suggest that bow and arrow technology was used earlier on the Plains than it was on the Canadian or Columbia Plateaus.

Material culture similarities between the Northwest Coast and the Canadian Plateau are evident in this cultural horizon, as in preceding horizons. Small side-notched points similar to the Kamloops side-notched points are present in the *Esilao phase* (ca. 750–150 BP) of the Lower Fraser River (Borden 1968:23) and the *Stselax phase* (ca. 700–150 BP) of the Fraser Delta (Borden 1970:110, Figure 33). Small, chipped stone side-notched points and corner-notched, barbed points are found in Component 2 of the Belcarra Park site on the Southern Northwest Coast, dating between ca. 1600 and 1000 BP (Charlton 1980). Small side-notched points are also found in late prehistoric contexts on the Central Northwest Coast (Carlson 1972, 1976).

Exchange with the Northwest Coast continued throughout the Kamloops horizon, with nephrite, vitreous basalt, obsidian and steatite being traded from the Mid-Fraser River region to the southern Coast (see Borden 1968; Charlton 1980; Wilmeth 1973); and slate, whalebone, and shells of coastal origin being traded into the interior (Sanger 1968a).

PLATEAU PITHOUSE TRADITION

The three prehistoric cultural horizons described above have a strong continuity in culture traits and patterns, and constitute the ***Plateau Pithouse tradition*** (ca. 4000/3500 to 200 BP) (Figures 3 and 14). The general pattern of lifeway during the Plateau Pithouse tradition is similar to that described for the ethnographic Interior Salish (Boas 1890; Dawson 1891; Teit 1900, 1906, 1909, 1930). The Plateau Pithouse tradition is characterized by the use of semi-subterranean pithouses as winter dwellings in semi-permanent villages, a semi-sedentary settlement pattern, a hunting and gathering mode of subsistence with a strong emphasis on salmon fishing, and storage of food in earth cellars (storage pits).

Suprisingly few details are known about subsistence practices during the Plateau Pithouse tradition, although it is apparent that deer, elk, a variety of small mammals, salmon, non-anadromous fish, fresh water mussels, birds and an assortment of gathered roots and berries formed the basic diet. The relative importance of hunted, fished, or gathered food resources varied from region to region and between horizons. In considering the "forager-collector" subsistence and settlement organizational strategy continuum proposed by Binford (1980), the Plateau Pithouse tradition fits the description of the logistical or "collector" pattern.

While differences between cultural horizons are evident, these differences constitute variations on a common cultural theme. Cultural elements/patterns shared by all three horizons are:

1. use of pithouses as winter dwellings;

2. use of earth cellars as food storage facilities and a hypothesized reliance on stored food in winter;

3. hypothesized semi-sedentary settlement pattern involving permanent winter settlements, and short-term non-winter resource extraction and/or processing camps and stations;

4. reliance on anadromous salmon as the primary food, supplemented by large and small land mammals, fresh water fish and mussels, birds, and wild plant resources;

5. use of earth ovens at pithouse sites for baking or roasting food;

6. use of a heavy-duty woodworking tool kit consisting of nephrite adzes, bone and antler wedges, and large hammerstones or hand mauls;

7. a sophisticated bone and antler fishing technology;

8. emphasis on chipped stone tools;

9. limited use of ground stone tools;

10. anthropomorphic and zoomorphic carving in stone;

11. hypothesized wood and plant fibre industry (e.g., basketry, matting,

cordage, projectile weaponry, handles, wedges, etc.);

12. use of stone boiling technique for cooking (probably with bark or basketry containers); and

13. exchange with Northwest Coast cultures involving nephrite and steatite going to the coast, with marine shells being traded to the interior.

Cultural differences between horizons include:

1. changes in the form and size of pithouses, which may be related to aspects of social organization (Stryd 1971; Richards and Rousseau 1982; Hayden *et al* 1985);

2. changes in the size of storage pits and earth ovens, and their positioning relative to pithouses;

3. variation in emphasis on wild root resource exploitation (see Pokotylo and Froese 1983);

4. increased exchange with the Northwest Coast (Fladmark 1982);

5. a shift from primary reliance on local lithic raw materials to the increased use of extra-local raw materials;

6. changes in projectile point styles, and diminution of average point size through time;

7. change in the dominant hunting weapon system technology from spear and/or atlatl to the bow and arrow;

8. variation in the quality of chipped stone workmanship;

9. increased importance of the ground stone tool industry;

10. increased frequency in stone and antler sculpture;

11. increased frequency of bone and antler tool decoration;

12. elaboration of the bone and antler industries; and

13. changes in burial modes.

Paleoclimatic studies conducted on the Canadian and Columbia Plateaus (Hansen 1955; Alley 1976; Hebda 1982; King 1980; Mack, Rutter, and Valastro 1978; Campbell 1985a; Mathewes 1984) indicate that from ca. 8000 to 4500 BP the climate was slightly warmer and drier than present (Figure 14). Sometime between ca. 4500 and 4000 BP cool and moist conditions were established, followed shortly by the commencement of the Plateau Pithouse tradition between 4000 and 3500 years ago. Modern climatic conditions were established between ca. 3000 and 2000 BP, characterized by warm and dry conditions.

Cultural changes during the Plateau Pithouse tradition may be attributable to several factors, including: (1) minor environmental changes and consequent cultural re-adaptation (i.e., the onset of slightly warmer and drier conditions sometime between 3000 and 2000 BP may be related to the shift from the Shuswap to Plateau horizons); (2) increasing adaptive efficiency to a reasonably stable environment; (3) adaptive changes related to increasing human population density; and 4) adaptation to a changing socio-cultural environment, perhaps related to southward Athapaskan migratory pressure (see Wilmeth 1978b; Magne and Matson 1984:301-365, 1985), or socio-economic pressures exerted by the more highly developed Northwest Coast cultures to insure a reliable supply of Canadian Plateau nephrite and steatite (Fladmark 1982:131,135).

During the Plateau Pithouse tradition there is a general pattern of sustained cultural continuity, although the horizons are recognized and defined as variations on a basic cultural adaptive theme. Continuity in human population and ethnicity is suggested by the data. Since people occupying the Canadian Plateau at the time of contact were primarily Interior Salish, it is likely that the Plateau Pithouse tradition represents the prehistory of this ethno-linguistic group. Other researchers have also postulated long-standing population/cultural continuities on the Canadian Plateau (e.g., Sanger 1970:127; Stryd 1973b:30,31). A late prehistoric southward migration of Athapaskans onto the northwestern Canadian Plateau is also apparent (see Wilmeth 1978b; Magne and Matson 1984, 1985), but the repercussions of this event or process are as yet poorly understood.

DISCUSSION AND SUMMARY

One important question raised in this synthesis is: to what degree did the inhabitants of the Mid-Fraser River region (Boston Bar to Big Bar Creek) participate in Canadian Plateau cultural horizons? It appears that during the Shuswap horizon, cultural patterns in this region were much like those noted for the rest of the Canadian Plateau. During the following Plateau and Kamloops horizons, however, this region diverged to some degree with respect to other regions. The most salient difference is in housepit size—on average they are substantially larger than elsewhere. This may be attributable, in part, to significant differences in social organization. It has been hypothesized that important cultural developments in the Mid-Fraser River region involved changes in social organization and intensification of interaction with coastal cultures between ca. 2000 and 1000 BP (see Stryd 1971, 1973a, 1974; Fladmark 1982; Hayden *et al* 1985).

Hayden *et al* (1985) postulate that large late prehistoric housepits (greater than 15 m in diameter) in the Lillooet and mouth of the Chilcotin localities were occupied by large socioeconomic coresidential "corporate groups" who had exclusive control over certain important resources or trading rights, whereas smaller dwellings (9 to 15 m) were occupied by socioeconomic units of lesser importance. They argue that the larger average size of Mid-Fraser River region housepits compared to those found elsewhere on the Canadian Plateau (see Tables 4 and 5) may indicate the existence of corporate groups resulting from trade contacts with the Northwest Coast.

The only single component excavated Shuswap horizon housepit from the Lillooet locality (HP 1, EeRk 4) is 16.4 m in diameter, which is 4.8 m larger than any other single component Plateau or Kamloops horizon housepit from this locality. Like elsewhere on the Canadian Plateau, it may be that the use of very large housepits was also common in the Lillooet locality during the Shuswap horizon, and therefore, it is possible that many of these large houses may simply owe their size to adaptive or behavioral factors which are unrelated to the existence of corporate groups. This may be especially true of large multi-component pithouse sites which span the entire Plateau Pithouse tradition. If such is the case, we caution that the provisional identification of "corporate group" pithouses simply on the basis of large house diameters might be erroneous in some instances.

In considering the small sample (n = 5) of single component excavated Plateau horizon housepits from the Mid-Fraser Region (Table 5), they are considerably larger than elsewere on the Canadian Plateau, having a mean diameter of 9.9 m (s.d. = 1.72; range = 8.0 to 11.6 m). This phenomenon may be due to the existence of "corporate group" behavior as hypothesized by Hayden *et al* (1985), although this remains to be demonstrated. House dimensions during this time appear to be similar to those for the later single component Kamloops horizon dwellings in this region (n = 6), which have a mean diameter of 9.48 m (s.d. = 1.32 m, range = 7.5 to 11.2 m). The Mid-Fraser River region Kamloops horizon houses have diameters similar to those from other regions of the Canadian Plateau during this time.

Fladmark (1982:131) suggests that on the Canadian Plateau there appears to have been a ". . . marked peak of cultural deposition about 1000–1500 BP . . .

perhaps indicating some kind of climax in the number and size of pit-house settlements at this time." This statement was based upon his plotting of radiocarbon dates by 100-year increments, and the assumption that ". . . the frequency of dated site/levels may be a rough measure of the relative density of aboriginal occupation through time" (Fladmark 1982:115). This assumption is questionable because of the non-representative manner in which most investigations have been carried out; and because of the biased nature of the archaeological record, in which older sites are under-represented due to erosion in the river valleys where most pithouse villages were located. To test Fladmark's hypothesis, we plotted all currently available radiocarbon dates by 100-year increments, but we have distinguished Mid-Fraser River region dates from those derived from sites located elsewhere on the Canadian Plateau (Figure 24; Table 13). Mid-Fraser River region dates definitely cluster between 1000 and 1500 BP, but the dates from the rest of the Canadian Plateau are not exceptionally frequent during this period and instead reflect a general increase in numbers through time.

Another important question is: to what extent did prehistoric Athapaskan Chilcotin, Lower Carrier, and Nicola populations participate in the Plateau Pithouse tradition? To properly answer this, it is important to know precisely when these groups or their ancestors appeared on the Canadian Plateau. At Tezli, located in ethnographic Lower Carrier territory, Donahue (1978) sees cultural and population continuity for over 4000 years without evidence for any disruptive influx. It is possible that ancestral Lower Carrier Athapaskans were partially acculturated to the Plateau Pithouse tradition and occupied the area for thousands of years.

A socio-ecological model proposing a southward intrusion of Chilcotin Athapaskans has recently been advanced by Magne and Matson (1984:301-365, 1985). They propose that as a result of the White River volcanic eruption, there was a southward influx of northern Athapaskan groups between ca. 1250 and 650 BP which passed through south-central B.C. (see also Wilmeth 1978b; Workman 1978). A "tension zone" between Athapaskan and Salishan groups is hypothesized to have existed around 450 years ago with the southern extent of winter villages occupied by small Athapaskan groups located in the approximate vicinity of Anahim Lake (Magne and Matson 1984:360, 1985; Wilmeth 1978b). Such a tension zone would no doubt have resulted in greater contact between the western Shuswap and Chilcotin commencing around 450 BP. Several ethnographic accounts mention that there was frequent interaction between these two culture groups (i.e., through intermarriage, trade, warfare) (see Lane 1953; Morice 1893; Ray 1939; Teit 1909). Available archaeological and ethnographic evidence suggest that the Plateau Athapaskans were at least partially acculturated to the primarily Salishan Plateau Pithouse tradition.

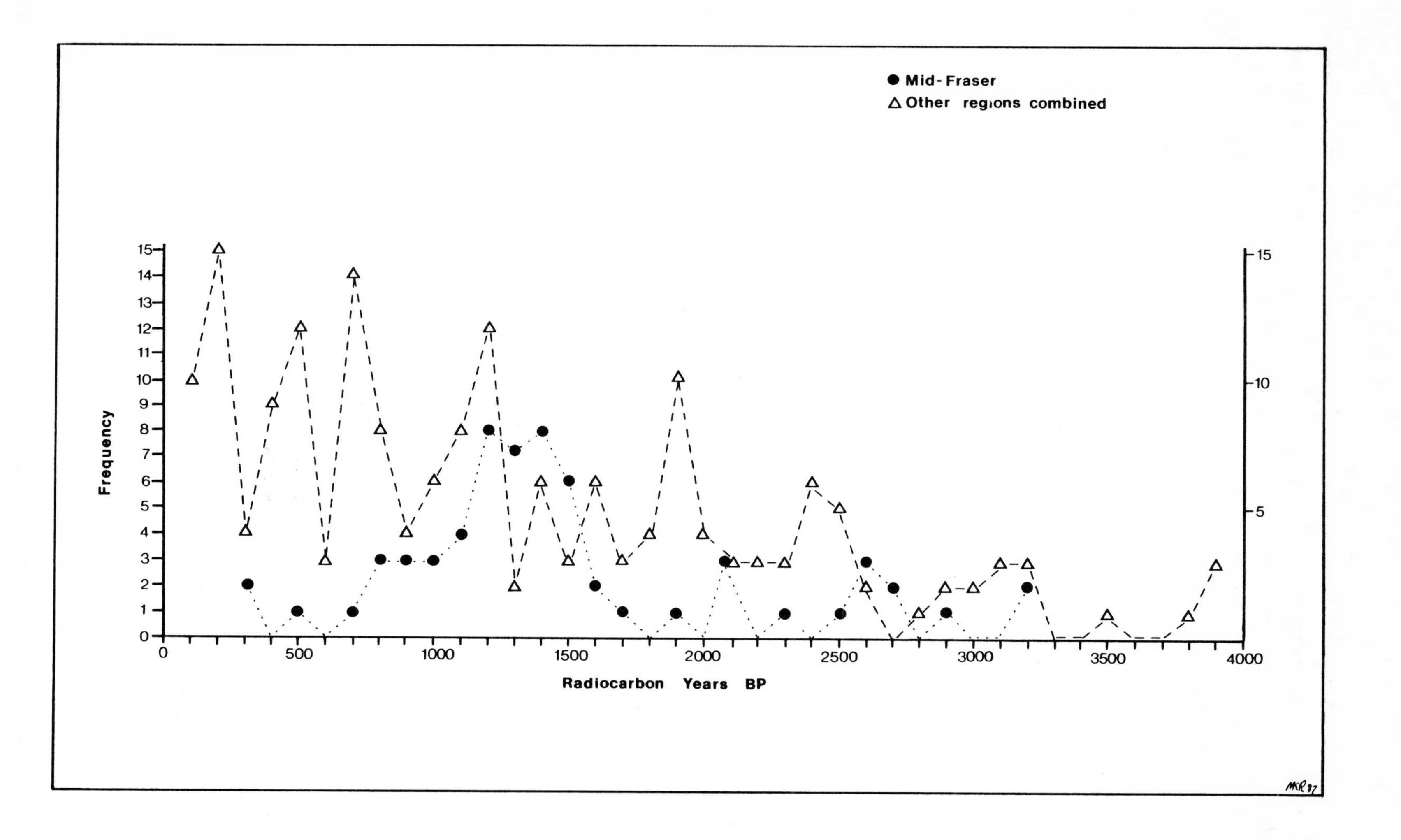

Figure 24. Frequencies of radiocarbon dates secured from Plateau Pithouse tradition components plotted in 100-year intervals for the last 4000 years (see Tables 12 and 13). The solid dots represent Mid-Fraser River region dates only; the triangles are all other regions combined.

The Nicola-Similkameen are recognized as being a small group of Athapaskans who arrived relatively late on the Interior Plateau, and occupied the Nicola and Similkameen Valleys as far south as the mouth of the Similkameen River in Washington (see Bouchard and Kennedy 1984:12-22). The duration of Athapaskan Nicola-Similkameen occupation in this area remains controversial and poorly understood. Dawson (1891:24) and MacKay (1899:74-75) maintain that they arrived in the mid-1700s as a result of a Chilcotin war expedition against the Shuswap, whereas Boas (1895:31-33) argues that they had occupied the area for much longer. On the basis of linguistic evidence, Wyatt (1972:196) suggests that Athapaskan occupation of the Nicola Valley began after ca. 600 BP. Archaeological research directed at identifying prehistoric Athapaskan (Nicola-Similkameen) occupation of the Nicola Valley produced inconclusive results (Wyatt 1972:196). Perhaps future archaeological research will help to resolve this important problem.

In spite of a considerable amount of research conducted on the Canadian Plateau over the last 25 years, subsistence and settlement patterns are still very poorly understood. Most researchers make extensive recourse to analogy with Interior Salish ethnographic data. For example, house depressions from prehistoric sites are often described by archaeologists as the remains of winter habitations, but this assumption is never substantiated by analysis of floral or faunal seasonal indicators. It is possible that some housepits were occupied during other seasons, or perhaps even year-round. Also, salmon have been widely regarded as the most important food resource throughout most of the Canadian Plateau in late prehistoric times. Until recently, this assessment has been based entirely on ethnographic analogy. The archaeological evidence surely does indicate that salmon was a major food resource throughout the Plateau Pithouse tradition, however, fluctuations or major changes in its relative importance or proportion respective to other food resources has yet to be properly examined.

In order to determine the dietary importance of individual mammal, bird, or plant species, detailed faunal and floral analyses must be undertaken. Such studies are rarely conducted as standard procedure in Canadian Plateau sites, and we strongly emphasize that this situation must change. Detailed study of faunal assemblages from sites widely separated in space and time will probably only provide a general picture of Canadian Plateau subsistence. What is desperately needed to gain an understanding of Plateau Pithouse tradition subsistence/settlement patterns is a regional approach as advocated by Binford (1964). We believe that this approach would be facilitated by the use of regionally defined phase sequences.

Following a model of Upper Columbia drainage basin settlement dynamics recently posited by Choquette (1985), Lawhead, Stryd, and Curtin (1986:31-32) have hypothesized that there may have been a decreased availability of salmon during the Plateau horizon compared to the earlier Shuswap horizon and later Kamloops horizon as a direct result of changing climatic conditions. They suggest that the decline in this important resource may have been offset to some degree by an increase in the intensification of upland root and plant resources, and increased group mobility. An overall population decline throughout the Plateau horizon is also postulated. Alternately, we hypothesize that although salmon may have decreased slightly at that time, we regard the Plateau horizon as a period of probable population increase in relation to the Shuswap horizon. Resource stresses imposed by growing numbers of people, and perhaps a reduction in salmon numbers, may have been offset by simply expanding the repertoire of resource options, and/or by intensifying the use of secondary resources (i.e., upland roots, berries and game), a readaptive strategy that may not have detrimentally affected population growth. Carbon isotope ($\delta^{13}C$) analysis of an adequate sample of Plateau and Shuswap horizon skeletons would be useful in determining if in fact there was a notable decrease in the relative quantity of dietary marine protein.

A major problem in Canadian Plateau archaeology involves microblade technology. The formal and technological attributes of microblades and cores have been documented as the "Plateau Microblade tradition" (Sanger 1968c), although many microblade assemblages lack some of the characteristics of this technological tradition as described by Sanger (see Ludowicz 1983:11; Campbell 1985b:299–304). It has been hypothesized that this tradition originated in the northwestern Subarctic area and spread southward either through population migration or diffusion (see Sanger 1967:191, 1968c:112, 1970:127; Borden 1969:2, 1979:967). The Plateau Microblade tradition remains poorly understood, and we are presently uncertain about its commencement and termination dates, spatial distribution, function, and cultural significance (see Sanger 1967; Donahue 1975, 1978; Stryd 1973a; Fladmark 1982; Borden 1979: Wilmeth 1978b; Helmer 1977a,b).

In a recent assessment of microblade technology on the Columbia Plateau, Campbell (1985b:299–304) notes that it is represented between ca. 7000 to 3000 BP in the Rufus Woods Lake region, and it is evident only at temporary field camps and resource procurement stations/locations and not at winter village/base camp sites. Ludowicz's (1983:153–164) study of Lochnore–Nesikep locality and Upper Hat Creek Valley microblade assemblages concludes that microblades were more common at lithic scatter base camps than winter pithouse settlements. We concur with Campbell (1985b:301) that the presence and frequency of microblades at a site are most probably related to functional considerations arising from specific activities and their executive strategies, rather than being indicative of ethnic affiliation. Microblades are represented in notably high frequencies at upland sites immediately adjacent to small lakes and/or streams (see Pokotylo and Froese 1983; Stryd and Lawhead 1983; Lawhead, Stryd, and Curtin 1986). Some researchers hypothesize that the apparent high density of microblade sites observed in upland areas adjacent to the Thompson River valley may be indicative of Athapaskan presence (see Lawhead, Stryd, and Curtin 1986:190; Magne and Matson 1985:18). Adequate sampling and investigation of upland resource procurement sites should be conducted in many regions on the Canadian Plateau to examine this important problem in greater depth. A regional approach involving the investigation of various types of contemporaneous sites will undoubtedly help to solve the "microblade problem".

Pictographs and petroglyphs have not been discussed in this synthesis due to the present inability to date them by absolute means, although we think that they are late prehistoric phenomena. The dating of pictographs may be possible by the Accelerator Mass Spectrometer (AMS) method (Nelson, Korteling, and Stott 1977) if uncontaminated organic binding constituents of the paint can be recovered.

In conclusion, this study is a synthetic summary and general culture–historical framework that will facilitate the chronological ordering of archaeological data in localities or regions on the Canadian Plateau that are currently unknown or poorly understood. The horizons are to be considered as Canadian Plateau-wide archaeological integrative units which should be useful for general levels of comparison with other archaeological areas. This synthesis will hopefully permit archaeologists conducting research on the Canadian Plateau to speak a common language, and allow us to begin addressing problems relating to culture process and adaptation.

REFERENCES CITED

Alley, N.F.
1976 The palynology and paleoclimatic significance of a dated core of Holocene peat, Okanagan Valley, British Columbia. *Canadian Journal of Earth Sciences* 13:1131-1141.

Ames, Kenneth M. and Alan G. Marshall
1980 Villages, demography and subsistence intensification on the southern Columbia Plateau. *North American Archaeologist* 2(1):25-52.

Ames, Kenneth M., James P. Green and Margaret Pfoertner
1981 *Hatwai (10NP143) Interim Report.* Archeological Reports No. 9, Boise State University, Boise Idaho.

Archer, David J. W.
1980 Analysis of Spatial Patterns at a Prehistoric Settlement in the Lower Fraser Canyon, B.C. Unpublished M.A. Thesis, Department of Anthropology, University of British Columbia, Vancouver.

Bicchieri, Barbara
1975 Units of culture and units of time: periodization and its use in syntheses of Plateau preshistory. *Northwest Anthropological Research Notes* 9(2):246-265.

Binford, Lewis R.
1964 A consideration of archaeological research design. *American Antiquity* 31(2):203-210.

1965 Archaeological systematics and the study of culture process. *Amercian Antiquity* 31(2):203-210.

1968 Some comments on historical versus processual archaeology. *Southwestern Journal of Anthropology* 24:267-75.

1980 Willow smoke and dog's tails: hunter-gatherer settlement systems and archaeological site formation. *American Antiquity* 45:4-20.

Blake, Michael T.
1974 The explanation of late prehistoric settlement pattern variation in the Thompson and Fraser River valleys, British Columbia. *BC Perspectives* 5:1-17.

1976 *The Rocky Point Site (EdQx 20): Spatial Analysis and Descriptive Report.* Occasional Papers of the Archaeological Sites Advisory Board of British Columbia, Victoria.

Blake, Michael T. and Morley Eldridge
1971 Final Report on the Excavation of Pemberton Village, EeQx 2. Report on file, Heritage Conservation Branch, Victoria.

Boas, Franz
1890 The Shuswap. *Report of the British Association for the Advancement of Science* 1886–1889:632–647.

1895 The Tinneh Tribe of the Nicola Valley. *Fifth Report on the Indians of British Columbia, British Association for the Advancement of Science, Annual Report*, pp. 30–34.

Borden, Charles E.
1951 Results of a Preliminary Survey of the Nechako Reservoir in West Central British Columbia. Report on file, Heritage Conservation Branch, Victoria.

1952 Results of archaeological investigations in central British Columbia. *Anthropology in British Columbia* 3:31–40.

1961 *Fraser River Archaeological Project.* Anthropology Papers, No. 1. National Museum of Canada, Ottawa.

1968 Prehistory of the lower mainland. In *Lower Fraser Valley: Evolution of a Cultural Landscape*, edited by A. Siemens, pp. 9–26. B.C. Geographical Series 9, Dept. of Geography, University of B.C.

1969 Early population movements from Asia into western North America. *Syesis* 2:1–13.

1970 Culture history of the Fraser Delta region: an outline. In *Archaeology in British Columbia, New Discoveries*, edited by R. L. Carlson, pp. 95–112. B.C. Studies, Special Issue 6–7.

1979 Peopling and early cultures of the Pacific Northwest. *Science* 203(4384):963–871.

Bouchard, Randy and Dorothy Kennedy
1984 *Indian History and Knowledge of the Lower Similkameen River – Palmer Lake Area, Okanagan County, Washington.* Technical report submitted to the U.S. Army Corp of Engineers, Seattle District.

1985 Lakes Indian Ethnography and History. Manuscript on file, Heritage Conservation Branch, Victoria.

Brumley, John
1980 Salvage excavations within Cypress Hills Provincial Park. In *Archaeology in Alberta 1979*, edited by P. F. Donahue. Archaeological Survey of Alberta, Occasional Paper No. 15.

Burley, David V.
1980 *Marpole. Anthropological Reconstructions of a Prehistoric Northwest Coast Culture Type.* Department of Archaeology, Simon Fraser University, Publication 8, Burnaby.

Bussey, B. Jean
1977 The Comparison of Lithics at Three Sites in the East Kootenay Area of British Columbia. Unpublished M.A. thesis, Dept. of Archaeology, Simon Fraser University, Burnaby.

1983 Alexis Creek Archaeological Investigations. Report on file, Heritage Conservation Branch, Victoria.

Caldwell, Joseph R.
1958 *Trend and Tradition in the Prehistory of the Eastern United States.* American Anthropological Association, Memoir 88.

Caldwell, Warren W.
1966 The Middle Missouri tradition reappraised. *Plains Anthropologist,* 11(32):152–157.

Caldwell, Warren W. and Oscar L. Mallory
1967 *Hells Canyon Archaeology.* Smithsonian Institution River Basin Surveys Publications in Salvage Archaeology No. 6.

Campbell, J.M.
1968 The Kavik site of Anaktuvuk Pass, Arctic Alaska. *Anthropological Papers of the University of Alaska* 14:32–42.

Campbell, Sarah K.
1985a Sedimentary sequence at excavated sites and regional paleoenvironmental reconstruction. In *Summary of Results, Chief Joseph Dam Cultural Resources Project, Washington,* edited by S. Campbell, pp. 149–178. Manuscript on file, Office of Public Archaeology, Institute for Environmental Studies, University of Washington, Seattle.

1985b Selected aspects of the artifact assemblage. In *Summary of Results, Chief Joseph Dam Cultural Resources Project, Washington,* edited by S. Campbell, pp. 289–316. Manuscript on file, Office of Public Archaeology, Institute for Environmental Studies, University of Washington, Seattle.

1985c Discussion and conclusions. In *Summary of Results, Chief Joseph Dam Cultural Resources Project, Washington,* edited by S. Campbell, pp. 483–514. Manuscript on file, Office of Public Archaeology, Institute for Environmental Studies, University of Washington, Seattle.

1985d *Summary of Results, Chief Joseph Dam Cultural Resources Project, Washington* (ed.) Manuscript on file, Office of Public Archaeology, Institute for Environmental Studies, University of Washington.

Carlson, Catherine
1980 Excavations at the Curr site. In *The Archaeology of Kamloops,* by R.L. Wilson and C. Carlson, pp. 87–123. Department of Archaeology, Simon Fraser Univeristy Publication 7.

Carlson, Roy L.

1970 Excavations at Helen Point on Mayne Island. In *Archaeology in British Columbia, New Discoveries*, edited by R. L. Carlson, pp. 113–125. B.C. Studies, Special Issue 6–7.

1972 Excavations at Kwatna. In *Salvage '71*, edited by R. L. Carlson, pp. 41–58. Department of Archaeology, Simon Fraser Univeristy, Publication 1.

1976 The 1974 excavations at McNaughton Island. In *Current Research Reports*, edited by R. L. Carlson, pp. 99–114. Department of Archaeology, Simon Fraser University, Publication 3.

Chance, David H., and J.V. Chance

1977 *Kettle Falls 1976: Salvage Excavations in Lake Roosevelt.* University of Idaho Anthropological Research Manuscript Series 39.

1979 *Kettle Falls: 1977.* University of Idaho, Anthropological Research Manuscript Series 69.

1982 *Kettle Falls: 1971/1974.* University of Idaho, Anthropological Research Manuscript Series 69.

Charlton, Arthur S.

1980 *The Belcarra Park Site.* Department Archaeology, Simon Fraser University, Publication 9.

Chatters, James C.

1984 *Human Adaptation Along the Columbia River, 4700–1600 BP. A Report on Test Excavations at River Mile 590, North Central Washington.* Central Washington University, Graduate Studies and Research, Research Reports, 84–1. Ellensburg.

Chisholm, Brian S.

1986 Reconstruction of Prehistoric Diet in British Columbia Using Stable–Carbon Isotopic Analysis. Ph.D Dissertation, Simon Fraser University.

Chisholm, Brian S. and D. Erle Nelson

1983 An early human skeleton from south–central British Columbia: Dietary inference from carbon isotopic evidence. *Canadian Journal of Archaeology* 7(1):85–86.

Choquette, Wayne

1981 The role of lithic raw material studies in Kootenay archaeology. In Fragments of the Past: British Columbia Archaeology in the 1970s, edited by K. R. Fladmark, pp. 21–36. *BC Studies* 48.

Choquette, Wayne (continued)
1984 A proposed cultural chronology for the Kootenai region. In *Cultural Resource Investigations of the Bonneville Power Administration's Libby Integration Project, Northern Idaho and Northwestern Montana*, edited by S. Gough, pp. 303–316. Archaeological and Historical Services Eastern Washington University Reports in Archaeology and History, 100–29.

1985 Salvage Excavations at DiQj–18: A Test of a Model of Upper Columbia Basin Human Settlement Dynamics. Report on file, Heritage Conservation Branch, Victoria.

Copp, Stanley A.
1979 Archaeological Excavations at the McCall Site, South Okanagan Valley, British Columbia. Unpublished M.A. thesis, Department of Archaeology, Simon Fraser University.

Curtin, A. Joanne and Stephen Lawhead
1985 Spallumcheen Heritage Inventory Project: Pinaus Lake Burial Salvage (1984). Report on file, Heritage Conservation Branch, Victoria.

Clague, J.J.
1981 *Late Quaternary Geology and Geochronology of B.C. Part 2: Summary and Discussion of Radiocarbon Dated Quaternary History.* Geological Survey of Canada Paper 80–35.

Clark, David L.
1968 *Analytical Archaeology.* Methuen and Co. Ltd., London.

Corliss, D.W.
1972 *Neck Width of Projectile Points: an Index of Culture Continuity and Change.* Idaho State University Museum, Occasional Papers 29.

Dalton, G.
1975 Karl Polanyi's analysis of long–distance trade and his wider paradigm. In *Ancient Civilizations and Trade*, edited by J. Sabloff and C. Lamberg–Karlovsky, pp. 63–132. University of New Mexico Press, Albuquerque.

Dawson, George M.
1891 Notes on the Shuswap People of British Columbia. *Transactions of the Royal Society of Canada. 1st Series* 9(2):3–44.

Donahue, Paul F.
1975 Concerning Athapaskan prehistory in British Columbia. *Western Canadian Journal of Anthropology* 5(3–4):21–63.

1978 4500 Years of Cultural Continuity on the Central Interior Plateau of British Columbia. Unpublished Ph.D. dissertation, Department of Anthropology, University of Wisconson, Maddison.

Duff, Wilson
1952 *The Upper Stalo Indians of the Fraser River of B.C.* Anthropology in British Columbia, Memoir 1. B.C. Provincial Museum, Victoria.

Dyck, Ian
1983 The Prehistory of Southern Saskatchewan. In *Tracking Ancient Hunters: Prehistoric Archaeology in Saskatchewan,* edited by Henry T. Epp and Ian Dyck, pp. 63–139. Regina: Saskatchewan Archaeological Society.

Eldridge, Morley
1974 *Recent Archaeological Investigations near Chase, B.C.* Cariboo College Papers in Archaeology 2, Kamloops.

1982 Archaeological Spatial Analysis of DiRi 14. Unpublished M.A. Thesis, Department of Anthropology, University of Victoria.

1984 Vallican Archaeological Site (DjQj 1): A Synthesis and Management Report. Report on file, Heritage Conservation Branch, Victoria.

Eldridge, Morley and Arnoud H. Stryd
1983 CN Rail Railyard Expansion Project Heritage Mitigation Study Kamloops Junction, B.C. Report on file, Heritage Conservation Branch, Victoria.

Fladmark, Knut F.
1976 Punchaw Village: A preliminary report. The archaeology of a prehistoric settlement. In *Current Research Reports,* edited by R. L. Carlson, pp. 19–32. Department of Archaeology, Simon Fraser University, Publication 3.

1978 Concave side-scrapers: possible horizon markers in the Intermontane West. Paper presented at the 11th Annual Meeting of the Canadian Archaeological Association, Quebec.

1982 An introduction to the prehistory of British Columbia. *Canadian Journal of Archaeology* 6:95–156.

1984 Mountain of glass: archaeology of the Mount Edziza obsidian source, British Columbia, Canada. *World Archaeology* 16(2):139–156.

1985 *Glass and Ice: The Archaeology of Mt. Edziza.* Department of Archaeology Simon Fraser University Publication No. 14, Burnaby.

Forbis, Richard G.
1960 Some late sites in the Oldman River region, Alberta. *National Museum of Canada Bulletin 162, Contributions to Anthropology, 1957.*

Galdikas-Brindamour, Birute
1972 Faunal material from eight archaeological sites: A preliminary report. In *Salvage '71,* edited by R. L. Carlson, pp. 199–205. Department of Archaeology, Simon Fraser University, Publication 1.

Godfrey-Smith, Dorothy I.
1985 X-ray Flourescence Characterization of the Obsidian Flows From the Mount Edziza Volcanic Complex of British Columbia, Canada. Unpublished M.A. Thesis, Department of Archaeology, Simon Fraser University.

Goggin, John M.
1949 Culture traditions in Florida prehistory. In *The Forida Indian and his Neighbours*, edited by John W. Griffin, pp. 13-44. Winter Park, Florida.

Grabert, Garland F.
1968 *North-central Washington prehistory.* University of Washington, Department of Anthropology, Reports in Archaeology 1.

1970 Prehistoric Cultural Stability in the Okanagan Valley of Washington and British Columbia. Unpublished Ph.D. dissertation, University of Washington.

1974 Okanagan archaeology: 1966-1967. *Syesis* 7, supplement 2.

Greengo, Robert E.
1982 *Studies in Prehistory, Priest Rapids and Wanapum Reservoir Areas, Columbia River, Washington.* Report of U.S. Department of Interior, National Park Service, San Francisco. Unviersity of Washington, Department of Anthropology.

1986 *Prehistory of the Priest Rapids - Wanapum Region, Columbia River, Washington.* BAR International Series 290.

Gryba, Eugene M.
1980 Highway Archaeological Salvage Projects in Alberta. Report on file, Archaeological Survey of Alberta, Edmonton.

Ham, Leonard
1975 Shuswap Settlement Patterns. Unpublished M.A. thesis, Department of Archaeology, Simon Fraser University.

Hansen, H. P.
1955 Postglacial forests in south-central and central British Columbia. *American Journal of Science* 253:640-658.

Hanson, Gordon W.
1973 The Katz Site: A Prehistoric Pithouse Settlement in the Lower Fraser Valley, British Columbia. Unpublished M.A. Thesis, Department of Anthropology and Sociology, University of British Columbia.

Hayden, Brian, D. Alexander, K. Kusmer, D. Lepofsky, D. Martin, M. Rousseau, and P. Friele

1986 Report on the 1986 Excavations at Keatley Creek: A Report of the Fraser River Investigations Into Corporate Group Archaeology Project. Report on file, Department of Archaeology, Simon Fraser University, Burnaby.

Hayden, Brian, Morley Eldridge, Anne Eldridge, and Aubrey Cannon

1985 Complex Hunter-Gatherers in Interior British Columbia. In *Prehistoric Hunter-Gatherers*, pp. 181-199. Academic Press.

Hebda, Richard J.

1982 Postglacial history of grasslands of Southern British Columbia and adjacent regions. In *Grassland Ecology and Classification Symposium Proceedings June 1982*, pp. 157-192.

Helmer, James

1977a Site dispersal in the Blackwater Valley: Theoretical perspectives and preliminary synthesis. In *Annual report for the year 1975. Activities of the Archaeological Sites Advisory Board of B.C. and selected research reports*, edited by B. Simonson, pp. 46-107. Heritage Conservation Branch, Victoria.

1977b Points, people and prehistory: A preliminary synthesis of culture history in north central British Columbia. In *Prehistory of the North American subarctic: The Athapaskan Question*, edited by J. Helmer, S. Vandyke and F. Kense, pp. 90-96. University of Calgary Archaeological Association.

Hill-Tout, Charles

1903 Ethnological studies of the mainland Halkomelem, a division of the Salish of British Columbia. *Report of the 72nd meeting of the British Association for the Advancement of Science*, Belfast, Sept. 1902, pp. 355-449.

Holmes, Brian G.

1966 The Schaake Site: A New Study. Unpublished M.A. thesis, University of Washington.

Jermann, Jerry V.

1985 *Archaeological Inventory and Testing of Prehistoric Habitation Sites, Chief Joseph Dam Project, Washington.* University of Washington, Office of Public Archaeology for U.S. Army Corps of Engineers, Seattle District.

Johnson-Fladmark, Sharon

1973 Shuswap Lakes Archaeological Project. Report on file, Heritage Conservation Branch, Victoria.

Kenny, Ray
1972 Preliminary Report Deep Creek Site (FbRn 13). Report on file, Heritage Conservation Branch, Victoria.

King, Miriam
1980 Palynological and Macrofossil Analyses of Lake Sediments From the Lillooet Area, British Columbia. Unpublished M.Sc. thesis, S.F.U.

Kroeber, Alfred L.
1939 *Cultural and Natural Areas of Native North America.* University of California Publications in American Archaeology and Ethnology 38, Berkley.

Kusmer, Karla D.
1984 Heritage Investigations on Tsinstikeptum Indian Reserve Number 10: Analysis of Faunal Remains From the 1984 Excavations. Manuscript on file, Heritage Conservation Branch, Victoria.

Laforet, Andrea and Annie York
1981 Notes on the Thompson winter dwelling. In *The World is as Sharp as a Knife: An Anthology in Honour of Wilson Duff,* edited by D. Abbott, pp. 115–112. British Columbia Provincial Museum.

Lane, R.B.
1953 Cultural Relations of the Chilcotin Indians of West-Central British Columbia. Unpublished Ph.D. dissertation, University of Washington.

Lawhead, Stephen
1979 Salvage Archaeology Project: Investigations in Six Locations in British Columbia. Report on file, Heritage Conservation Branch, Victoria.

Lawhead, Stephen and Arnoud H. Stryd
1985 Excavations at the Rattlesnake Hill Site (EeRh 61), Ashcroft, B.C. Manuscript on file, Heritage Conservation Branch, Victoria.

Lawhead, Stephen, Arnoud H. Stryd, and A. Joanne Curtin
1986 Archaeological Excavations at Valley Mine, Highland Valley, B.C. Report on file, Heritage Conservation Branch, Victoria.

Leaming, S.
1971 *Rock and Mineral Collecting in British Columbia.* Geological Survey of Canada Paper 72-53.

Lehmer, Donald J. and Warren W. Caldwell
1966 Horizon and tradition on the Northern Plains. *American Antiquity* 31(4):511-516.

Leonhardy, Frank C. and David G. Rice
1970 A proposed culture typology for the lower Snake River region, southeastern Washington. *Northwest Anthropological Research Notes* 4(1):1-29.

Lohse, Ernest S.
1985 Rufus Woods Lake projectile point chronology. In *Summary of results, Chief Joseph Dam cultural resources project, Washington,* edited by S. Campbell, pp. 317–364. Manuscript on file, Office of Public Archaeology, Institute for Environmental Studies, University of Washington, Seattle.

Lovell, Nancy C.
1982 Isotopic Determination of Dietary Habits of Prehistoric Inhabitants of the British Columbia Interior. Unpublished B.A. Honors Essay, Department of Archaeology, Simon Fraser University.

Lovell, Nancy C., Brian S. Chisholm, D. Erle Nelson and Henry P. Schwarcz
1983 Proportions of marine species protein in the diet of prehistoric British Columbia interior dwellers. Paper presented at the XIth International Congress of Anthropological and Ethnological Sciences, Vancouver.

Ludowicz, Deanna
1983 Assemblage Variation Associated with Southwestern Interior Plateau Microblade Technology. M. A. Thesis, Department of Anthropology and Sociology, University of British Columbia, Vancouver.

Mack, R.N., N.W. Rutter, and S. Valastro
1978 Late Quaternary pollen record from the Sanpoil River Valley, Washington. *Canadian Journal of Botany* 56:1642–1650.

MacKay, John
1899 The Indians of British Columbia. *The B.C. Mining Record, Supplement,* 1899.

MacNeish, Richard S.
1978 *The Science of Archaeology?* Duxbury Press, Massachusetts.

Magne, Martin P.R.
1984 Taseko Lakes Prehistory Project: Report on a Preliminary Survey. Report on file, Heritage Conservation Branch, Victoria.

Magne, Martin and R.G. Matson
1984 Athapaskan and Earlier Archaeology at Big Eagle Lake, British Columbia. Manuscript on file, Archaeology Laboratory, University of British Columbia.

1985 A preliminary model of Athapaskan movements on the Interior Plateau of British Columbia. Paper presented at the 1985 meetings of the Canadian Archaeological Association, Winnipeg.

Mathewes, Rolf W.
1984 Paleobotanical evidence for climatic change in southern British Columbia during the late–glacial and Holocene time. In Climatic Change in Canada 5, edited by C.R. Harrington. *Syllogeus* 55:397–422.

Matson, R.G., M. Magne, D. Ludowicz, and D.L. Pokotylo
1980 The Eagle Lake Project: Report on the 1979 Season. Manuscript on file, Laboratory of Archaeology, University of British Columbia, Vancouver.

Matson, R.G., L.C. Ham, and D.E. Bunyan
1981 Prehistoric Settlement Patterns at the Mouth of the Chilcotin River, B.C. Report on file, Heritage Conservation Branch, Victoria.

McLeod, Ann and Mark Skinner
1987 Analysis of Burial 86-6 from the Fountain Creek Site (EeRl 19), near Lillooet. Report on file, Heritage Conservation Branch, Victoria.

McMurdo, Ann
1972 A Typological Analysis of Barbed Bone and Antler Projectile Points From the Northwest Coast. Unpublished M.A. thesis, Department of Archaeology, Simon Fraser University.

Mitchell, Donald H.
1963 Esilao — A Pit House Village in the Fraser Canyon, British Columbia. Unpublished M.A. Thesis. Department of Anthropology and Sociology, University of British Columbia.

1970 Archaeological investigations on the Chilcotin Plateau, 1968. *Syesis* 3:45-65.

1971 Archaeology of the Gulf of Georgia area, a natural region and its culture types. *Syesis* 4, Supplement 1.

Mohs, Gordon
1980a Shuswap Planning Study. The Heritage Resources of the Western Shuswap Basin. An Inventory, Interpretation, and Evaluation. Report on file, Heritage Conservation Branch, Victoria.

1980b Excavations of a Rectangular Housepit, Heritage Site EdQs 14. Report on file, Heritage Conservation Branch, Victoria.

1981 *An Assessment and Evaluation of Heritage Resources in the South Thompson River Valley of British Columbia.* Heritage Conservation Branch Occasional Paper 8, Victoria.

1982 Final Report on Excavations at DjQj 1, Slocan Valley, British Columbia. Report on file, Heritage Conservation Branch, Victoria.

Montgomery, Pamela
1978 Stone Artifacts From the Punchaw Lake Site (Area C): A Late Prehistoric Occupation in Central British Columbia. Unpublished M.A. thesis, Department of Archaeology, Simon Fraser University.

Morice, Adrian G.
1893 Notes archaeological, industrial, and sociological on the Western Denes. *Transactions of the Canadian Institute 4:1-222.*

Morlan, R. E.
1973 *The Later Prehistory of the Middle Porcupine Drainage, Northern Yukon Territory.* National Museum of Man Mercury Series, Archaeological Survey of Canada Paper No. 11.

Nelson, D. Erle and Keith Hobson
1982 Simon Fraser Radiocarbon Dates No. I. *Radiocarbon,* 24(3):344–351.

Nelson, D. Erle, R. G. Korteling, and W. R. Stott
1977 Carbon-14: Direct Detection at Natural Concentrations. *Science,* 198:507–508.

Nelson, D. Erle and G. Will
1976 Obsidian sources in the Anahim Peak area. *Current Research Reports,* edited by R. L. Carlson, pp. 151–154. Simon Fraser University Department of Archaeology Publication No. 3.

Nelson, Charles M.
1969 *The Sunset Creek Site (45-KT-28) and its Place in Plateau Prehistory.* Laboratory of Anthropology, Washington State University, Report of Investigations 47, Pullman.

Neuman, Robert W.
1975 *The Sonota Complex and Associated Sites on the Northern Great Plains.* Nebraska State Historical Society Publications in Anthropology No. 6. Lincoln.

Palmer, Gary B.
1975 Cultural ecology in the Canadian Plateau: Pre-contact to the early contact period in the territory of the southern Shuswap Indians of British Columbia. *Northwest Anthropological Research Notes* 9(2):199–245.

Phillips, Philip and Gordon R. Willey
1953 Method and theory in American archaeology: An operational basis for culture-historical integration. *American Anthropologist* 55:615–33.

Pokotylo, David L. and Patricia D. Froese
1983 Archaeological evidence for prehistoric root gathering on the southern Interior Plateau of British Columbia: A case study from Upper Hat Creek Valley. *Canadian Journal of Archaeology* 7(2):127–157.

Pokotylo, David L., Marian E. Binkley, and A. Joanne Curtin
1987 *The Cache Creek Burial Site (EeRh 1), British Columbia.* British Columbia Provincial Museum Contributions to Human History No. 1.

Quigg, J. Michael
1981 Highway mitigation program: 1980. In *Archaeology in Alberta 1980*, edited by J. Brink. Archaeological Survey of Alberta, Occasional Paper No. 17.

Ray, Verne F.
1939 *Cultural Relations on the Plateau of Northwestern America*. Publications of the Frederick Webb Hodge Anniversary Publication Fund, Vol. 3. Los Angeles.

Reeves, B.O.K.
1969 The Southern Alberta Paleo - Cultural Paleo Environmental Sequence. In *Post-Pleistocene Man and His Environment on the Northern Plains*, pp. 6–46. University of Calgary Archaeological Association, Calgary.

1974a Prehistoric archaeological research on the eastern slopes of the Canadian Rocky Mountains, 1967–1971. *Canadian Archaeological Association Bulletin* 6:1–29.

1974b *Crowsnest Pass Archaeological Project 1972: Salvage Excavations and Survey*. Archaeological Survey of Canada Paper No. 19. Ottawa.

1983 *Culture Change in the Northern Plains: 1000 B.C.- A.D. 1000*. Archaeological Survey of Alberta, Occasional Paper 20, Edmonton.

Rice, David G.
1972 *The Windust Phase in Lower Snake River region prehistory*. Washington State University, Laboratory of Anthropology, Reports of Investigations 50.

Richards, Thomas H.
1977 Typology of Projectile Points Recovered by the Lillooet Archaeological Project. Manuscript in possession of the author.

1978 Excavations at EeRl 171. Report on file, Heritage Conservation Branch, Victoria.

1982 Salvage Excavations at the Chinook Cove Site (EhRa 10), North Thompson River, British Columbia. Report on file, Heritage Conservation Branch, Victoria.

1983 Analysis of Faunal Remains From Six Okanagan Valley Archaeological Sites. Manuscript on file, Westbank Indian Council, Westbank.

1984 A Preliminary Examination of Prehistoric Northern Plains—Canadian Plateau/Southern Northwest Coast Trade Relationships. Manuscript in possession of the author.

1987 Microwear Patterns on Experimental Cache Creek Basalt Tools. Unpublished M.A. thesis, Department of Anthropology and Archaeology, University of Saskatchewan, Saskatoon.

Richards, Thomas H. and Mike K. Rousseau
1982 Archaeological Investigations on Kamloops Indian Reserve No. 1, Kamloops, British Columbia. Ms. on file, Heritage Conservation Branch, Victoria.

1983 The later prehistory of the Canadian Plateau. Paper presented at the XIth International Congress of Anthropological and Ethnological Sciences, Vancouver.

Roberts, Gerry W.
1974 The Inkameep Archaeology Project. Report on file, Heritage Conservation Branch, Victoria.

Rousseau, Mike K.
1982 An Interpretive and Descriptive Analysis of Lithic Artifacts From Site DjQj 1, Vallican, Slocan Valley, British Columbia. Manuscript on file, Heritage Conservation Branch, Victoria.

1984a Heritage Investigations on Tsinstikeptum Indian Reserve Number 10, Westside Locality, North Okanagan Valley, British Columbia. Report on file, Heritage Conservation Branch, Victoria.

1984b A Preliminary Report on the Activities and Findings of the Westbank Indian Council Heritage Project–Phase II: A General Heritage Site Inventory, Excavation Summaries, and Recommendations for Site Management. Report on file, Heritage Conservation Branch, Victoria.

1985 List of radiocarbon dates in possession of the author for excavated sites in the Westside locality of the North Okanagan Valley.

Rousseau, Mike K. and Geordie Howe
1979 Test Excavations at DhQv 6, South Okanagan Valley, British Columbia. Report on file, Heritage Conservation Branch, Victoria.

Rousseau, Mike K. and Thomas Richards
1985 A culture–historical sequence for the South Thompson River–Western Shuswap Lakes Region of British Columbia: the last 4000 years. *Northwest Anthropological Research Notes* 19(1):1–32.

Rutherford, A. A., J. Wittenburg, and R. Wilmeth
1981 University of Saskatchewan Radiocarbon dates IX. *Radiocarbon* 23 (1):94–135.

Rutherford, A. A., J. Wittenburg, and B. C. Gordon
1984 University of Saskatchewan Radiocarbon dates X. Radiocarbon 26(2):241–292.

Sammons-Lohse, Dorothy
1985 Features. In *Summary of Results, Chief Joseph Dam Cultural Resources Project, Washington,* edited by S. Campbell, pp. 455–480. Manuscript on file, Office of Public Archaeology, Institute for Environmental Studies, University of Washington.

Sanger, David
1967 Prehistory of the Pacific Northwest as seen from the Interior of British Columbia. *American Antiquity* 32(2):186–197.

1968a The Chase burial site in British Columbia. *National Museum of Canada Bulletin* 224:86–185, Ottawa.

1968b *The Texas Creek Burial Site Assemblage, British Columbia.* National Museum of Canada, Anthropology Paper 17, Ottawa.

1968c Prepared core and blade traditions in the Pacific Northwest. *Arctic Anthropology* 5(1):92–120.

1969 Cultural traditions in the interior of British Columbia. *Syesis* 2:189–200.

1970 The archaeology of the Lochnore–Nesikep locality, British Columbia. *Syesis* 3, Supp. 1:1–129.

Sendey, John
1972 Preliminary Report of Excavations at Site EfQu 3, Shuswap Lake Provincial Park, 1971. Report on file, Heritage Conservation Branch, Victoria.

Schalk, R. F. and G. Cleveland
1983 A sequence of adaptations in the Columbia–Fraser Plateau. In *Cultural Resources Investigation for the Lyons Ferry Fish Hatchery Project, near Lyons Ferry, Washington,* edited by R. Schalk. Washington State University Laboratory of Archaeology and History, Project Report 8.

Skinner, Mark and Stanley S. Copp
1986 The Nicoamen River Burial Site (EbRi 7), Near Lytton, British Columbia. Report on file, Heritage Conservation Branch, Victoria.

Smith, Harlan I.
1900 *Archaeology of the Thompson River Region.* Memoirs of the American Museum of Natural History 2:6. New York.

Stapp, Darby C.
1984 Late Protohistoric Burials With Copper Artifacts in the Pacific Northwest. Unpublished M.A. thesis, University of Idaho.

Stryd, Arnoud H.

1971 An archaeological research design for the investigation of pithouse anthropology. In *Aboriginal Man and Environments on the Plateau of Northwest America*, edited by A.H. Stryd and R.A. Smith, pp. 36–43. University of Calgary Archaeological Association.

1972 Housepit archaeology at Lillooet, British Columbia: the 1970 Field Season. *B.C. Studies* 14:17–46.

1973a The Later Prehistory of the Lillooet Area, British Columbia. Ph.D. Dissertation, University of Calgary, Calgary.

1973b The later prehistory of the Canadian Plateau. Paper presented at the 6th annual meeting of the Canadian Archaeological Association, Burnaby.

1974 *Lillooet Archaeological Project: 1974 Field Season.* Cariboo College Papers in Archaeology 1, Kamloops.

1980 A review of the recent activities undertaken by the Lillooet Archaeological Project. *The Midden* 12(2):5–20.

1981a The 1980 Investigations of the Monte Creek Archaeological Site (EdQx 15). Report on file, Heritage Conservation Branch, Victoria.

1981b Prehistoric sculptures from the Lillooet area of British Columbia. *Datum* 6(1):9–15.

1983a An overview of Lillooet prehistory: the last 4500 years. Paper presented at the XIth International Congress of Anthropological and Ethnological Sciences, Vancouver.

1983b Prehistoric mobile art from the mid-Fraser and Thompson River areas. In *Indian Art Traditions of the Northwest Coast*, edited by R.L. Carlson, pp. 167–181. Archaeology Press, Simon Fraser University.

Stryd, Arnoud H. and Stephen Lawhead

1978 *Reports of the Lillooet Archaeological Project Number 1. Introduction and Setting.* Archaeological Survey of Canada, Mercury Series 73.

1983 Bethlehem Copper Corporation Lake Zone Development Heritage Mitigation Study. Report on file, Heritage Conservation Branch, Victoria.

Swanson, E.H. Jr.

1962 *The Emergence of Plateau Culture.* Idaho State College Museum, Occasional Papers 8.

Teit, James A.
1900 The Thompson Indians. *American Museum of Natural History Memoirs* 2:4, New York.

1906 The Lillooet Indians. *American Museum of Natural History Memoirs* 2(5):195–292, New York.

1909 The Shuswap. *American Museum of Natural History Memoirs* 4:7. New York.

1930 The Salishan Tribes of the Western Plateaus. *Annual Reports of the Bureau of American Ethnology* 45:295–396, Washington.

Turnbull, Christopher J.
1977 *Archaeology and Ethnohistory in the Arrow Lakes, Southeastern British Columbia.* Archaeological Survey of Canada, Mercury Series 65, Ottawa.

Thomas, D. H.
1978 Arrowheads and atlatl darts: how the stones got the shaft. *American Antiquity* 43:461–472.

Vickers, Roderick
1986 *Alberta Plains Prehistory: A Review.* Archaeological Survey of Alberta, Occasional Paper No. 27. Edmonton.

Von Krogh, Henning
1976 The 1974 Katz Salvage Project. In *Current Research Reports,* edited by R. L. Carlson, pp. 68–82. Department of Archaeology Simon Fraser University, Publication No. 3.

1978 Archaeological Investigations in the Spences Bridge Locality, British Columbia. Report on file, Heritage Conservation Branch, Victoria.

1980 *Archaeological Investigations at the Flood and Pipeline Sites, near Hope, British Columbia.* Occasional Papers of the Heritage Conservation Branch 4, Victoria.

Warren, Claude N.
1968 *The View From Wenas: A Study of Plateau Prehistory.* Occasional Papers of the Idaho State University Museum 24.

Whitlam, Robert G.
1976 *Archaeology in the William's Lake Area, British Columbia.* Occasional Papers of the Archaeological Sites Advisory Board of British Columbia 1, Victoria.

1980 *Archaeological Investigations at Cache Creek (EeRh 3).* Occasional Papers of the Heritage Conservation Branch, No. 5, Victoria.

Willey, Gordon R.
1966 *An Introduction to American Archaeology, Volume One: North and Middle America.* Englewood Cliffs, New Jersey, Prentice–Hall.

1971 *An Introduction to American Archaeology, Volume Two: South America.* Englewood Cliffs, New Jersey, Prentice–Hall.

Willey, Gordon R. and Philip Phillips
1958 *Method and Theory in American Archaeology.* University of Chicago Press, Chicago.

Wilmeth, Roscoe
1973 Distribution of several types of obsidian from archaeological sites in British Columbia. *Canadian Archaeological Association Bulletin* 5:27–60.

1978a *Canadian Archaeological Radiocarbon Dates (revised version).* Archaeological Survey of Canada, Mercury Series, Paper 77.

1978b *Anahim Lake Archaeology and the Early Historic Chilcotin Indians.* Archaeological Survey of Canada, Mercury Series, Paper 82.

1980 Excavations at the Nakwantlun Site (FdSi 11) in 1980. Report on file, Heritage Conservation Branch, Victoria.

1981 Excavations at the Nakwantlun Site (FdSi 11) in 1981. Report on file, Heritage Conservation Branch, Victoria.

Wilson, Robert L.
1980 Archaeological investigations near Kamloops. In *The Archaeology of Kamloops,* by R. Wilson and C. Carlson, pp. 1–83. Department of Archaeology, Simon Fraser University, Publication 7.

1983 North Thompson River Archaeological Project Report No. 2: Heritage Resource Investigations of the Mid–North Thompson River Region, British Columbia. Report on file, Heritage Conservation Branch, Victoria.

Wormington, H. Marie and Richard G. Forbis
1965 *An Introduction to the Archaeology of Alberta, Canada.* Denver Museum of Natural History, Proceedings, No. 11. Denver.

Workman, William B.
1978 *Prehistory of the Aishihik–Kluane Area, Southwest Yukon Territory.* Archaeological Survey of Canada, Mercury Series, Paper 74.

Wyatt, David J.
1971 A preliminary outline of Nicola Valley prehistory. In *Aboriginal Man and Environments on the Plateau of Northwest America,* edited by A.H. Stryd and R.A. Smith, pp. 60–72. University of Calgary Archaeological Association.

Wyatt, David J. (continued)
1972 The Indian History of the Nicola Valley, British Columbia. Unpublished Ph.D. dissertation, Deptartment of Anthropology, Brown University.

Zeier, Charles D.
1982 The Willey and Phillips system revisited: A proposed expansion of the paradigm. *Plains Anthropologist* 27(95):29–36.

Table 1. Sites containing excavated components attributed to the Shuswap horizon (ca. 4000/3500-2400 BP).

Site Number	Location	Component Type*	Fig. 15	References
DiQm 1	Arrow Lakes	HP	-19	Turnbull 1977
DiQm 4	" "	HP	-18	" "
DiQw 2	North Okanagan	LS	-17	Grabert 1974
DlQv 37	" "	LS	-16	Rousseau 1984a
DlQv 39	" "	LS	-16	" "
EbRc 6	Nicola Lake	LS	-13	Wyatt 1971,1972
EcRh 11	Thompson River	HP	-12	Von Krogh 1978
EdRk 4	Lochnore-Nesikep	LS	-10	Sanger 1970
EdRk 7	" "	HP	-11	" "
EdRk 8	" "	HP	-11	" "
EdRk 9	" "	HP/B	-11	" "
EeRb 10	Kamloops locality	HP	-14	Wilson 1980; Richards and Rousseau 1982
EeRk 4	Lillooet locality	HP	-8	Stryd 1972,1973a,1980
EeRl 7	" "	HP	-7	Hayden et al 1986
EeRl 22	" "	HP	-9	Stryd 1972,1973a,1980
EfQu 3	Shuswap Lake	HP/B	-15	Sendey 1972
FaRx 1	Chilanko River	LS	-5	Mitchell 1970
FbRn 13	Williams Lake	HP	-6	Kenny 1972
FdSi 11	Anahim Lake	HP	-4	Wilmeth 1980
FgSd 1	Tezli Lake	HP	-3	Donahue 1975,1978
FiRs 1	Punchaw Lake	DP/B	-2	Fladmark 1976
FiSi 19	Natalkuz Lake	HP	-1	Borden 1952

* HP=housepit; LS=lithic scatter; B=burial; DP=dwelling platform.

Table 2. Sites containing excavated components attributed to the Plateau horizon (ca. 2400-1200 BP).

Site Number	Location	Component Type*	Fig. 18	References
DiQj 5	Slocan Junction	HP	-34	Turnbull 1977
DiQm 4	Arrow Lakes	HP	-32	" "
DiQw 2	North Okanagan	HP	-30	Grabert 1974
DjQj 1	Slocan Valley	HP	-33	Eldridge 1984
DkQm 5	Arrow Lakes	HP	-31	Turnbull 1977
DlQv 37	North Okanagan	LS	-29	Rousseau 1984a
DlQv 52	" "	LS	-29	" "
EaRd 2	Nicola Valley	HP	-19	Wyatt 1971,1972
EbRc 3	" "	HP	-20	" " "
EbRh 1	" "	HP	-18	" " "
EcRh 1	" "	HP	-18	" " "
EcRh 11	Thompson River	HP	-17	Von Krogh 1978
EcRh 12	" "	CP/RP	-17	" " "
EcRg 2	Highland Valley	LS	-16	Stryd and Lawhead 1983
EcRg 4	" "	LS	-16	" " "
EcQt 2	North Okanagan	HP	-28	Grabert 1970,1974
EdRa 9	South Thompson R.	HP	-23	Wilson 1980
EdRa 22	Kamloops locality	HP	-23	Carlson 1980
EdRh 2	Thompson River	LS	-17	Von Krogh 1978
EdRk 8	Lochnore-Nesikep	HP	-15	Sanger 1970
EdRk 9	" "	HP	-15	" "
EdQx 5	South Thompson R.	HP	-24	Eldridge 1974
EdQx 15	" "	HP	-24	Stryd 1981a
EdQx 20	" "	HP	-24	Blake 1976
EeRa 4	Kamloops locality	HP	-23	Carlson 1980
EeRb 3	" "	HP	-22	Wilson 1980
EeRb 11	" "	HP	-22	" "
EeRb 68	" "	HP	-22	Eldridge and Stryd 1983
EeRb 70	" "	HP	-22	" " "
EeRc 44	" "	HP	-22	" " "
Government	" "	B	-22	Smith 1900
EeRj 1	Upper Hat Creek	RP	-14	Pokotylo and Froese 1983
EeRj 46	" " "	RP	-14	" " "
EeRj 55	" " "	RP	-14	" " "
EeRj 71	" " "	RP	-14	" " "
EeRj 101	" " "	RP	-14	" " "
EeRk 4	Lillooet locality	HP/B	-11	Stryd 1972,1973a,1974,1980
EeRl 4	" "	HP	-13	" " " " "
EeRl 7	" "	HP	-10	Hayden *et al* 1986

continued

Table 2. (continued)

Site Number	Location	Component Type*	Fig. 18	References
EeRl 19	Lillooet locality	HP/B	-11	McLeod and Skinner 1987; Stryd 1972,1973a,1974,1980
EeRl 22	" "	HP	-12	" " " " "
EeQx 14	South Thompson R.	HP	-24	Eldridge 1974
EfQu 3	Shuswap Lake	HP	-26	Sendey 1972
EfQv 4	Adams River	LS	-25	Johnson-Fladmark 1973
EfQv 19	Shuswap Lake	HP	-27	" " "
EhRa 5	North Thompson R.	HP	-21	Wilson 1983
EhRv 2	Taseko Lakes	HP	-7	Magne 1984
EkSa 13	Eagle Lake	HP	-6	Magne and Matson 1984
EkSa 32	" "	HP	-6	" " "
ElRn 3	Williams Lake	HP	-9	Whitlam 1976
FaRn 3	" "	HP	-8	" "
FcSi 2	Anahim Lake	HP	-5	Wilmeth 1978b
FdSi 3	" "	HP	-3	" "
FdSi 11	" "	HP	-4	Wilmeth 1980
FgSd 1	Tezli Lake	HP	-2	Donahue 1975,1978
FiRs 1	Punchaw Lake	DP	-1	Fladmark 1976; Montgomery 1978

* HP=housepit; LS=lithic scatter; B=burial; RP=roasting pit; CP=cache pit; DP=dwelling platform.

Table 3. Sites containing excavated components attributed to the Kamloops horizon (ca. 1200-200 BP).

Site Number	Location	Component Type*	Fig. 21	References
DlQv 1	North Okanagan	LS	-42	Rousseau 1984a,1984b
DlQv 37	" "	LS	-42	" " "
DjQj 1	Slocan Valley	HP	-43	Eldridge 1984
EaRd 2	Nicola Valley	HP	-30	Wyatt 1972
EbRa 1	" "	HP	-31	" "
EbRa 2	" "	HP	-31	" "
EbRc 1	" "	HP	-30	" "
EbRg 1	" "	HP	-29	" "
EbRi 7	Nicoamen River	B	-28	Skinner and Copp 1986
EcRg 4	Highland Valley	LS	-26	Stryd and Lawhead 1983
EcRh 11	Thompson River	HP	-27	Von Krogh 1978
EcQt 2	North Okanagan	HP	-40	Grabert 1974
EcQv 2	" "	B	-39	Curtin and Lawhead 1985
EdQs 14	Shuswap River	HP	-41	Mohs 1980b
EdQx 15	S. Thompson River	HP	-36	Stryd 1981a
EdQx 20	" "	HP	-36	Blake 1976
EdRa 9	" "	HP	-35	Wilson 1980
EdRa 22	" "	HP	-35	Carlson 1980
EdRg 2	Highland Valley	LS	-26	Stryd and Lawhead 1983
EdRg 5	" "	LS	-26	" " "
EdRk 1	Texas Creek	B	-21	Sanger 1968b
EdRk 3	Lochnore-Nesikep	B	-23	Sanger 1970
EdRk 4	" "	LS	-22	" "
EdRk 5	" "	HP	-22	" "
EdRk 6	" "	HP	-22	" "
EeQw 1	S. Thompson River	B	-37	Sanger 1968a
EeQw 6	" "	HP	-37	Johnson Fladmark 1973
EeQw 15	" "	HP	-37	" " "
EeQw 64	" "	HP	-37	Blake and Eldridge 1971
EeQx 14	" "	HP	-36	Eldridge 1974
Large	Kamloops locality	B	-34	Smith 1900
EeRb 11	" "	HP	-34	Wilson 1980
EeRc 44	" "	HP	-34	Eldridge and Stryd 1983
EeRh 1	Cache Creek loc.	B	-25	Pokotylo et al 1987
EeRh 3	" " "	LS	-25	Lawhead 1979; Whitlam 1980
EeRj 1	Upper Hat Creek	RP	-24	Pokotylo and Froese 1983
EeRj 55	" " "	RP	-24	" " "
EeRk 4	Lillooet locality	HP	-16	Stryd 1972,1973a,1974,1980

continued

Table 3. (continued)

Site Number	Location	Component Type*	Fig. 21	References
EeRk 16	Lillooet locality	HP	-16	Stryd 1972,1973a,1974,1980
EeRl 4	" "	HP	-19	" " " " "
EeRl 6	" "	HP	-18	" " " " "
EeRl 7	" "	HP	-15	Hayden et al 1986
EeRl 19	Lillooet locality	HP/B	-16	Stryd 1972,1973a,1974,1980
EeRl 21	" "	HP	-20	" " " " "
EeRl 22	" "	HP	-17	" " " " "
EeRl 36	" "	HP	-18	" " " " "
EeRl 40	" "	HP	-16	" " " " "
EeRl 52	" "	HP	-15	" " " " "
EfQv 19	Shuswap Lake	HP	-38	Johnson Fladmark 1973
EhRa 5	North Thompson	HP	-33	Wilson 1983
EhRa 10	" "	LS	-33	Richards 1982
EiRa 3	" "	RP	-32	Wilson 1983
EiRb 5	" "	HP	-32	" "
EkRo 18	Mouth of Chilcotin	HP	-13	Matson, Ham, & Bunyan 1981
EkRo 31	" "	HP	-14	" " "
EkRo 48	" "	HP	-13	" " "
EkSa 13	Eagle Lake	HP	-8	Magne and Matson 1984
ElRn 3	Williams Lake	HP	-12	Whitlam 1976
ElRw 4	Chilco River	HP	-10	Matson et al 1980
C.R. 73	" "	HP	-9	" " "
C.R. 92	" "	LS	-9	" " "
FaRt 16	Alexis Creek	LS/RP	-11	Bussey 1983
FaRt 17	" "	CP/RP	-11	" "
FcSi 1	Anahim Lake	HP	-6	Wilmeth 1978b
FcSi 2	" "	HP	-6	" "
FdSi 2	" "	HP	-5	Mitchell 1970
FdSi 11	" "	HP	-7	Wilmeth 1980
FgSd 1	Tezli Lake	HP	-3	Donahue 1975,1978
FiRs 1	Punchaw Lake	DP	-4	Fladmark 1976;Montgomery 1978
FiSi 2	Euchu Lake	LS	-2	Borden 1951
FiSi 19	Natalkuz Lake	HP	-1	Borden 1952

* HP=housepit; LS=lithic scatter; B=burial; RP=roasting pit; CP=cache pit; DP=dwelling platform.

Table 4. Diameters, depths and horizon affiliations of single component excavated housepits on the Canadian Plateau (excluding the Mid-Fraser River region).

Location	Site Number	House-pit	Average Dia.	Average Depth	Cultural Horizon*	References
Slocan Junction	DiQj 5	7	7.0	.75	P	Turnbull 1977
" "	"	8	7.5	.50	P	" "
Arrow Lakes	DiQm 1	2	9.0	.75	S	" "
" "	"	4	9.0	.40	S	" "
" "	DiQm 4	12	10.5	.40	S	" "
North Okanagan	DiQw 2	1	5.0	1.00	P	Grabert 1974
" "	EcQt 2	2	6.25	1.35	K	" "
Nicola Valley	EbRa 1	1	8.0	.50	K	Wyatt 1972
" "	"	2	8.5	.50	K	" "
" "	EbRa 2	1	12.0	.75	K	" "
" "	"	2	12.0	.75	K	" "
" "	EbRc 1	1	9.0	.65	K	" "
" "	EbRc 3	-	8.25	.75	P	" "
" "	EbRg 1	1	11.5	.75	K	" "
S. Thompson R.	EeRa 4	1	7.0	--	P	Carlson 1980
" "	EeRb 3	10	5.0	.35	P	Wilson 1980
" "	"	19	5.0	.15	P	" "
" "	"	22	6.0	.70	P	" "
" "	EeRb 11	1	6.5	--	P	" "
" "	EeRb 10	6	12.0	.90	S	Richards and
" "	"	7	10.0	.50	S	Rousseau 1982
" "	"	8	14.0	1.25	S	" "
" "	"	9	10.5	.60	S	" "
" "	"	1	8.8	.60	S	" "
" "	"	11	10.5	.75	S	" "
" "	"	14	7.6	.30	S	" "
" "	EeRb 68	6	7.25	.90	P	" "
" "	EeRb 44	20	7.25	.85	K	Eldridge and
" "	"	22	4.75	.30	P	Stryd 1983
" "	EeRb 70	11	5.0	.80	P	" "
" "	EdQx 15	7	9.0	.90	K	Stryd 1981a
" "	"	11	11.5	1.50	K	" "
" "	"	39	12.0	1.00	K	" "
" "	"	43	8.0	--	P	" "
" "	EdQx 20	A1	8.0	.50	P	Blake 1976
" "	EdRa 9	6	6.0	.70	K	Wilson 1980
" "	"	7	6.0	.85	K	" "
" "	"	9	7.0	1.00	K	" "

continued

Table 4. (continued)

Location	Site Number	House-pit	Average Dia.	Average Depth	Cultural Horizon*	References
S. Thompson R.	EdRa 22	1	6.5	.70	P	Carlson 1980
" "	"	6	5.5	.80	P	" "
" "	"	15	5.0	.40	P	" "
Shuswap Lake	EfQu 3	13	12.0	1.00	S	Sendey 1972
Shuswap River	EdQs 14	1	8.5	.35	K	Mohs 1980b
N. Thompson R.	EhRa 5	7	6.9	--	P	Wilson 1983
Chilcotin R.	EkRo 18	-	5.0	.40	P	Matson et al 1981
" "	EkRo 31	-	7.0	.25	K	" " "
Williams Lake	FbRn 13	-	16.0	1.80	S	Kenny 1972
Natalkuz Lake	FiSi 19	1	10.4	--	S	Borden 1952
Tezli	FgSd 1	D	10.0	--	S	Donahue 1975
Anahim Lake	FcSi 1	Bes Tco	5.0	.50	K	Wilmeth 1978b
" "	FdSi 1	Daniktco	7.5	.30	P	" "
Chilko River	CR # 73	1	9.5	--	K	Matson et al 1980
Eagle Lake	EkSa 32	1	4.5	--	P	Magne and Matson 1984
" "	"	2	4.0	--	P	

* S=Shuswap; P=Plateau; K=Kamloops.

Table 5. Diameters, depths and horizon affiliations of single component excavated housepits from the Mid-Fraser River region.

Location	Site Number	House-pit	Average Dia.	Average Depth	Cultural Horizon*	References
Lochnore-Nesikep	EdRk 6	1	9.5	.50	K	Sanger 1970
	EdRk 9	5	8.0	1.00	P	" "
Lillooet	EeRk 4	7	11.6	2.00	P	Stryd 1973a
"	"	1	16.4	2.60	S	" "
"	"	15	11.2	1.70	K	" "
"	"	21	10.4	.90	P	" "
"	EeRl 4	36	11.5	--	P	Stryd 1974
"	"	64	8.3	--	P	" "
"	EeRl 6	7	10.4	--	K	" "
"	"	9	7.5	--	K	" "
"	EeRl 21	16	9.8	--	K	" "
"	EeRl 36	10	8.5	--	K	" "

* S=Shuswap; P=Plateau; K=Kamloops.

Table 6. Metric attributes of Plateau Pithouse tradition projectile points. Measurements are from points recovered from sites located throughout the Canadian Plateau.

SHUSWAP HORIZON: All stylistic variants

Length (cm)				Width (cm)				Neck Width (cm)			
n	mean	s.d.	range	n	mean	s.d.	range	n	mean	s.d.	range
63	4.00	1.05	2.3-7.7	86	1.80	.30	1.1-2.9	59	1.10	.27	.6-2.0

PLATEAU HORIZON: Barbed spear/atlatl points

Length (cm)				Width (cm)				Neck Width (cm)			
n	mean	s.d.	range	n	mean	s.d.	range	n	mean	s.d.	range
57	4.10	1.03	2.8-7.1	50	2.60	.49	1.9-4.2	80	1.50	.34	.8-2.4

PLATEAU HORIZON: Barbed arrow points

Length (cm)				Width (cm)				Neck Width (cm)			
n	mean	s.d.	range	n	mean	s.d.	range	n	mean	s.d.	range
17	2.48	.53	1.7-3.5	24	1.73	.23	1.4-2.3	38	.73	.10	.5-.9

KAMLOOPS HORIZON: Side-notched arrow points

Length (cm)				Width (cm)				Neck Width (cm)			
n	mean	s.d.	range	n	mean	s.d.	range	n	mean	s.d.	range
53	2.04	.40	1.1-3.2	77	1.32	.23	.9-1.9	71	.72	.12	.4-1.0

KAMLOOPS HORIZON: Multi-notched arrow points

Length (cm)				Width (cm)				Neck Width (cm)			
n	mean	s.d.	range	n	mean	s.d.	range	n	mean	s.d.	range
10	2.94	.51	2.0-3.5	12	1.68	.33	1.1-2.0	18	.89	.19	.5-1.3

Table 7. Chipped stone artifact types present in investigated Plateau Pithouse tradition components.

Artifact Class/Type			Horizon Affilations		
			S	P	K*
BIFACES:					
Projectile Points					
eared:	lanceolate		+		
	corner-notched		+		
	side-notched		+		
stemmed:	parallel		+	+	
	expanding		+	+	
	contracting:	-large	+	+	+
		-small			+
barbed:	corner-notched:	-large			+
		-small		+	+
	basal-notched:	-large		+	
		-small		+	+
barbless:	lanceolate		+	+	
	leaf-shaped		+	+	+
	corner-notched		+	+	+
	side-notched:	-large			+
		-small			+
Preforms:	leaf-shaped		+	+	+
	triangular	-large			+
		-small			+
	lanceolate	-large	+	+	
		-small			+
	ovate		+	+	+
Drills:	side-notched				+
	expanding base			+	
	misc.		+	+	+
Other:	unformed flake tools		+	+	+
	unformed spall tools				+
	pentagonal bifaces				+
	key-shaped bifaces		+	+	

continued

Table 7. (continued)

Artifact Class/Type		Horizon Affilations S	P	K*
UNIFACES:				
Scrapers:	convex endscrapers	+	+	+
	end and side		+	+
	side		+	+
	thumbnail	+	+	+
	rectangular			+
	continuous		+	+
	hafted			+
	spall	+	+	
	split cobble	+	+	
	key-shaped unifaces	+	+	
Perforator/gravers:				
	narrow spurred		+	+
	wide spurred	+	+	
MICROBLADES/CORES:		+	+	
FLAKE CORES:	unidirectional	+	+	+
	multidirectional	+	+	+
	bipolar	+	+	+
UTILIZED FLAKE TOOLS:		+	+	+
OTHER/MISC.:	pendants			+
	eccentrics			+

* S=Shuswap; P=Plateau; K=Kamloops.

Table 8. Pecked and ground stone artifact types present in investigated Plateau Pithouse tradition components.

Artifact Class/Type		Horizon Affilations S	P	K*
ABRADERS:	shaft smoothers	+		+
	other	+	+	+
MAULS:	decorated		+	+
	undecorated		+	+
PESTLES:	decorated	+		
	undecorated	+		
CLUBS:	decorated			+
	undecorated			+
NET SINKERS:	notched	+		
	grooved		+	
	decorated		+	
ZOOMORPHIC FIGURINES:			+	+
BOWLS OR MORTARS:				+
NEPHRITE ITEMS:	celts -small ...	+	+	+
	-large ...		+	+
	celt blanks			+
	knives		+	+
SLATE ITEMS:	knives			+
	points			+
	pendants			+
	other/misc.		+	+
STEATITE ITEMS:	beads		+	+
	trumpet pipes		+	+
	zoomorphic figurines			+
	seated human figure bowls			+
	decorated bowls			+
	anthropomorphic pendants			+
	decorated rings			+
	decorated spindle whorls			+
	undecorated spindle whorls			+
HAMMERSTONES:		+	+	+
ANVILS:		+		

* S=Shuswap; P=Plateau; K=Kamloops.

Table 9. Bone artifact types present in investigated Plateau Pithouse tradition components.

Artifact Class/Type		Horizon Affilations		
		S	P	K*
COMPOSITE HARPOON VALVES:				
	self-armed		+	
	other			+
BEADS:	disc	+		
	oblong		+	
	tubular		+	+
POINTS:	unipoints	+	+	+
	bipoints	+	+	+
	unilaterally barbed	+	+	+
AWLS:	metapodial	+		
	splinter		+	+
	tibia			+
	cannon bone			+
	ulna			+
	other		+	+
BEAR PENIS BONES:	decorated/undecorated			+
OTHER:	gaming pieces			+
	mat creasers			+
	drinking tubes		+	+
	spoons	+		
	bracelets	+		
	eyed needles			+
	pins			+
	fish hook barbs			+
	three-stop whistles			+
	miniature bone bows			+
	zoomorph. whalebone clubs			+
	sap scrapers		+	+
	wedges	+		+
	scapula tools		+	

* S=Shuswap; P=Plateau; K=Kamloops.

Table 10. Antler, tooth, claw, and shell artifact types present in investigated Plateau Pithouse tradition components.

Artifact Class/Type		Horizon Affilations		
		S	P	K*
ANTLER:	composite harpoon valve	+	+	
	unipoint		+	+
	bilaterally barbed point	+	+	+
	unilaterally barbed point		+	+
	digging stick handle		+	+
	tine flaker	+	+	+
	wedge	+	+	+
	ring	+		
	haft		+	+
	club			+
	anthropomorphic figurines		+	+
	ornamental combs			+
	pendant			+
	sap scraper			+
	other	+	+	+
TOOTH:	beaver incisor gaming pieces			+
	ground incisor tools: -beaver		+	+
	-black bear			+
	-porcupine			+
	-marmot			+
	perforated teeth: -dog		+	
	-bear		+	
	-elk		+	+
	-deer		+	+
CLAW:	grooved bear claw	+		
	perforated claw: -eagle	+		
	-bear		+	
SHELL:	rattles: -*Pecten*		+	+
	-*Margeratifera*		+	+
	beads/pendants: -disc	+		
	-*Dentalia*		+	+
	-*Olivella*			+
	-*Pecten*			+
	-*Haliotis*			+
	serrated-edged object	+		
	unmodified shell: -*Dentalia*	+	+	+
	-*Olivella*			+

* S=Shuswap; P=Plateau; K=Kamloops.

Table 11. Identified faunal species present in investigated Plateau Pithouse tradition components.

Identified Faunal Species		Horizon Affilations		
		S	P	K*
MAMMALS:	elk	+	+	+
	mule deer	+	+	+
	white-tailed deer		+	+
	caribou		+	
	mountain sheep	+	+	+
	black bear	+	+	+
	cougar		+	
	wolf	+		
	coyote		+	
	domestic dog	+	+	+
	red fox	+		+
	marten		+	
	muskrat	+	+	
	beaver	+	+	+
	striped skunk	+		
	porcupine	+		
	snowshoe hare	+	+	+
	rabbit		+	+
	marmot			+
	woodchuck			+
	packrat			+
	western grey squirrel			+
	red squirrel			+
BIRDS:	duck	+		+
	grouse		+	+
	trumpeter swan	+		+
	red-necked grebe		+	
	common loon		+	
	Canada goose			+
	hooded merganser			+
	red-breasted merganser			+
	sandhill crane		+	
	saw-whet owl			+
	great horned owl		+	
	robin			+

continued

Table 11. (continued)

Identified Faunal Species		Horizon Affilations		
		S	P	K*
FISH:	trout	+	+	+
	salmon	+	+	+
	-pink		+	
	-spring ..			+
	-sockeye .			+
	other	+	+	+
FRESHWATER SHELLFISH:				
	Margaritifera falcata ...	+	+	+
	Anodonta grandis			+

* S=Shuswap; P=Plateau; K=Kamloops.

Table 12. Late prehistoric radiocarbon dates from Canadian Plateau sites. Each date is presented with one standard deviation of error. Horizon assessments are the opinions of the present authors.

Site Number	Site Name	Sample Type*	Date (BP)	Lab Number	Reference	Cultural Horizon**
Arrow Lakes Region						
DiQj 5	Slocan Junct.	C	1120+100	Gak 2899	Turnbull 1977	P
"	" "	C	1660+120	Gak 2900	" "	P
DiQm 1	Cayuse Creek	C	3150+170	Gak 2896	" "	S
"	" "	C	3215+120	GX 1197	" "	S
DiQm 4	Deer Park	C	2870+100	Gak 2897	" "	S
"	" "	C	2530+220	Gak 2898	" "	S
DjQj 1	Vallican	C	260+100	SFU 175	Mohs 1982	K
"	"	C	1250+120	SFU 177	" "	K
"	"	C	260+200	SFU 178	" "	K
"	"	C	480+200	SFU 179	" "	K
"	"	C	1040+110	SFU 180	" "	K
"	"	C	1780+80	SFU 181	" "	P
"	"	C	1170+260	SFU 182	" "	K
"	"	C	860+400	SFU 183	" "	K
"	"	C	790+150	SFU 184	" "	K
"	"	C	220+100	SFU 185	" "	K
"	"	C	980+250	SFU 186	" "	K
"	"	C	700+110	SFU 188	" "	K
"	"	C	1020+150	SFU 189	" "	K
"	"	C	1860+150	SFU 190	" "	P
"	"	C	750+90	SFU 191	" "	K
"	"	C	110+80	SFU 192	" "	K
"	"	C	700+100	SFU 193	" "	K
"	"	C	760+140	SFU 194	" "	K
"	"	C	2210+180	SFU 198	" "	P
DkQm 5	Inonoaklin	C	3090+200	Gak 2895	Turnbull 1977	S?
North Okanagan Valley						
DiQw 2	Marron Lake	C	2130+130	GSC 998	Grabert 1974	P
"	" "	B	2500+100	Gak 2335	" "	S
DlQv 1	Keefe Creek	C	1130+340	WSU 3061	Rousseau 1985	?
"	" "	C	3980+70	WSU 3062	" "	?
"	" "	C	540+70	WSU 3063	" "	K
"	" "	C	1095+60	WSU 3064	" "	?

continued

Table 12. (continued)

Site Number	Site Name	Sample Type*	Date (BP)	Lab Number	Reference	Cultural Horizon**
North Okanagan Valley (continued)						
DlQv 37	Siwash Point	C	1080±160	SFU 302	Rousseau 1984a	P?
DlQv 39	--	B	2370±80	WSU 3032	Rousseau 1985	S
DlQv 52	--	C	1900±80	SFU 351	Rousseau 1984a	P?
EcQt 2	Blattner	C	690±80	Gak 1894	Grabert 1974	K
South Thompson River-Western Shuswap Lakes Region						
EdQx 15	Monte Creek	C	450±80	SFU 32	Stryd 1981b	K
"	" "	C	200±80	SFU 33	" "	K
"	" "	C	530±80	SFU 34	" "	K
"	" "	C	1450±80	SFU 35	" "	P
"	" "	C	190±130	SFU 36	" "	K
"	" "	C	1760±130	SFU 37	" "	P
"	" "	C	1030±180	SFU 38	" "	K
EdRa 9	Harper Ranch	C	400±80	Gak 4914	Wilson 1980	K
"	" "	C	1950±130	Gak 4915	" "	P
"	" "	C	1140±100	Gak 4916	" "	K
EdRa 22	Curr	C	520±85	I 10032	Carlson 1980	K
"	"	C	2235±90	I 10033	" "	P
"	"	C	1995±190	I 10061	" "	P
"	"	C	490±80	I 10105	" "	K
"	"	C	385±80	I 10486	" "	K
"	"	C	1200±85	I 10487	" "	P
EeQw 6	Green Acres	C	560±70	S 757	Mohs 1981	K
"	" "	C	550±70	S 758	" "	K
"	" "	C	860±80	S 759	" "	K
"	" "	C	590±70	S 760	" "	K
EeRa 4	--	C	2085±80	I 10485	Carlson 1980	P
EeRb 3	Kamloops Reserve	C	1920±100	Gak 3902	Wilson 1980	P
EeRb 10	Van Male	B	3900±800	SFU 69	Richards and	S
"	" "	B	3000±400	SFU 70	Rousseau 1982	S
"	" "	B	2950±150	SFU 76	" "	S
"	" "	C	2950±120	SFU 104	" "	S
EeRb 70	--	C	1300±160	SFU 303	Eldridge and	P
"	--	C	1180±100	SFU 315	Stryd 1983	K
EeRc 44	--	C	2160±160	SFU 301	" "	P
"	--	C	2400±160	SFU 304	" "	P
"	--	C	280±80	SFU 315	" "	K

continued

Table 12. (continued)

Site Number	Site Name	Sample Type*	Date (BP)	Lab Number	Reference	Cultural Horizon**
South Thompson River-Western Shuswap Lakes (continued)						
EdQs 14	Shuswap River	C	490+130	SFU 50	Mohs 1980b	K
"	" "	C	870+180	SFU 51	" "	K
"	" "	C	430+100	SFU 56	" "	K
"	" "	A	980+100	SFU 57	" "	K
EfQu 3	Scotch Creek	C	3160+100	Gak 4262	Mohs 1980a	S?
"	" "	C	2540+100	Gak 4270	" "	S
EfQu 10	Blind Bay	C	3290+140	S 725	Wilmeth 1978a	?
"	Rockshelter	C	1695+165	S 726	" "	?
"	"	C	1485+90	S 727	" "	?
"	"	C	430+65	S 728	" "	?
EfQv 4	--	C	800+110	S 762	" "	K?
EfQv 19	Tate	C	1200+80	S 761	" "	P
Thompson River Region and Highland Valley						
EcRi 1	Drynoch Slide	C	3175+150	I 462	Wilmeth 1978a	?
EbRi 7	Nicoamen River	C	740+130	S 2696	Skinner and Copp 1986	K
EcRg 1B	--	C	210+60	Beta 13157	Lawhead, Stryd & Curtin 1986	?
EcRg 2AA	--	C	1120+170	SFU 230	" "	?
"	--	C	1490+150	SFU 219	" "	?
"	--	C	1920+210	SFU 231	" "	?
EdRg 1B	--	C	140+80	Beta 13158	" "	?
EeRh 1	Cache Creek	W	700+80	SFU 293	Pokotylo *et al* 1987	K
"	Burials	W	1330+260	SFU 227		K
"	"	W	760+110	SFU 228	" "	K
"	"	B	1960+400	SFU 292	" "	K?
Nicola Valley						
EbRc 3	Lake Corner	C	1980+140	Gak 3269	Wyatt 1972	P
EbRg 1	Matthew Washington	C	520+90	Gak 3285	" "	K

continued

Table 12 (continued)

Site Number	Site Name	Sample Type*	Date (BP)	Lab Number	Reference	Cultural Horizon**
Hat Creek Valley						
EeRj 1	--	C	970+60	S 1579	Pokotylo and Froese 1983	K?
"	--	C	2030+50	S 1580		P?
"	--	C	140+50	S 1582	" "	K?
EeRj 46	--	C	1550+60	S 1454	" "	P?
EeRj 55	--	C	1220+70	S 1455	" "	P?
"	--	C	600+40	S 1581	" "	K?
EeRj 71	--	C	2120+70	S 1453	" "	P?
"	--	C	2250+50	S 1642	" "	P?
EeRj 93	--	C	1270+140	SFU 277	" "	P?
EeRj 101	--	C	2090+70	S 1456	" "	P?
EeRk 42	--	C	1940+100	SFU 278	" "	P?
EeRk 43	--	C	2000+160	SFU 381	" "	P?
EeRk 53	--	C	790+120	SFU 280	" "	K?
"	--	C	700+100	SFU 365	" "	K?
Lochnore-Nesikep Locality						
EdRk 5	Cow Springs	C	310+30	GSC 405	Sanger 1970	K
"	" "	C	825+85	GSC 406	" "	K
"	" "	C	775+95	GX 406-2	" "	K
EdRk 7	Lochnore Creek	C	2670+130	GSC 407	" "	S
"	" "	C	2605+140	GSC 407-2	" "	S
"	" "	C	3280+125	GX 407	" "	S
"	" "	C	3220+90	GX 407-2	" "	S
"	" "	C	2680+100	I 1866	" "	S
"	" "	C	1610+95	I 2085	" "	?
EdRk 8	Lehman	C	2185+150	GSC 404	" "	?
Lillooet Locality						
EeRk 4	Bell	C	1515+90	I 6076	Stryd 1980	P?
"	"	C	1250+200	I 6076c	" "	P?
"	"	C	1590+90	I 6077	" "	P?
"	"	C	1420+200	I 6077c	" "	P?
"	"	C	2730+90	I 6633	" "	S
"	"	C	1010+80	I 9026	" "	K
"	"	C	1150+80	I 9027	" "	K?
"	"	C	1250+80	I 9028	" "	P?

continued

Table 12. (continued)

Site Number	Site Name	Sample Type*	Date (BP)	Lab Number	Reference	Cultural Horizon**
Lillooet Locality (continued)						
EeRk 4	Bell	C	1080+80	I 9561	Stryd 1980	K?
"	"	C	1325+80	I 9562	" "	P
"	"	C	1365+80	I 9563	" "	P
"	"	C	1100+80	I 9564	" "	K?
"	"	C	935+80	I 9569	" "	K
"	"	C	1155+80	I 9570	" "	K?
"	"	C	1295+80	I 9723	" "	P?
"	"	C	1495+80	I 9848	" "	K?P?
"	"	C	1930+70	S 659	" "	P?
"	"	C	1215+90	S 660	" "	K?
"	"	C	1560+90	S 661	" "	P?
"	"	C	1305+80	S 662	" "	P?
"	"	C	1380+65	S 709	" "	P?
"	"	C	1430+60	S 763	" "	P?
"	"	C	2965+95	S 764	" "	S?
"	"	C	1470+40	S 765	" "	P
"	"	C	1380+65	S 937	" "	P?
"	"	C	1575+145	S 938	" "	P?
EeRk 7	Gibbs Creek	C	920+90	Gak 3284	" "	K?
"	" "	C	1515+80	I 9029	" "	P?
EeRk 16	Lower Bell	C	1290+85	I 8060	" "	K?
EeRl 4	Bridge River	C	1380+85	I 8052	" "	P?
"	" "	C	1760+85	I 8053	" "	P
"	" "	C	1680+85	I 8054	" "	P
"	" "	C	1260+85	I 8055	" "	K?
"	" "	C	1495+80	I 9006	" "	P
"	" "	C	1150+80	I 9007	" "	K?
"	" "	C	1450+80	I 9008	" "	P
"	" "	C	1300+80	I 9571	" "	P?
EeRl 6	West Fountain	C	1260+85	I 8056	" "	K
"	" "	C	1075+85	I 8057	" "	K
EeRl 19	Fountain	C	1490+70	S 583	" "	P?
"	"	C	1505+70	S 584	" "	P?
"	"	B	1410+110	RIDDL 573	McLeod & Skinner 1987	P?

continued

Table 12. (continued)

Site Number	Site Name	Sample Type*	Date (BP)	Lab Number	Reference	Cultural Horizon**
Lillooet Locality (continued)						
EeRl 21	Seaton Lake	C	1220±85	I 8058	Stryd 1980	K?
"	" "	C	2360±90	I 8059	" "	P?
"	" "	C	2100±80	I 9009	" "	P?
"	" "	C	855±80	I 9010	" "	K
EeRl 22	Mitchell	C	2185±85	S 580	" "	P?
"	"	C	2550±80	S 581	" "	S?
"	"	C	2775±75	S 582	" "	S
EeRl 36	Squatter´s	C	520±80	I 9024	" "	K
"	"	C	980±80	I 9572	" "	K?
EeRl 40	East	C	395±80	I 9025	" "	K
EeRl 52	Sallus Creek	C	810±75	I10755	" "	K
Chilcotin Region						
EkSa 32	Boyd	C	505±70	WSU 2905	Magne and K	
EkSa 36	Bear Lake	C	295±75	WSU 2902	Matson 1984	K
EkRo 18	--	C	1290±80	Gak 5325	Matson *et al*	K?
EkRo 48	--	C	870±80	Gak 5326	1981	K
"	--	C	1450±75	Gak 5327	" "	P?
EkRo 87	--	C	770±65	Gak 5324	Ham 1975	K
ElRn 3	--	C	1660±85	Gak 4320	Whitlam 1976	P?
"	--	C	1860±85	Gak 4322	" "	P?
ElRw 4	Quiggly Holes	C	280±80	SFU 16	Matson *et al*	K
C.R. 73	--	C	360±80	SFU 15	" 1980	K
C.R. 92	--	C	860±80	SFU 14	" "	K
FaRn 3	Stafford Ranch	C	1290±80	Gak 4010	Whitlam 1976	P
"	" "	C	1770±100	Gak 4011	" "	P
"	" "	C	1210±100	Gak 4012	" "	P
FaRt 16	--	C	620±80	SFU 311	Bussey 1983	K
"	--	C	700±100	SFU 309	" "	K
FaRt 17	--	C	500±80	SFU 310	" "	K
FdSi 3	Daniktco	C	1247±57	BGS 84	Wilmeth 1978b	P
"	"	C	1251±57	BGS 85	" "	P
"	"	C	1110±160	Gak 3796	" "	P?
FcSi 1	Goose Point	C	710±80	S 502	" "	K?
"	" "	C	170±55	S 1037	" "	PH?
"	" "	C	245±75	S 1038	" "	PH
"	" "	C	790±205	S 1039	" "	K?

continued

Table 12. (continued)

Site Number	Site Name	Sample Type*	Date (BP)	Lab Number	Reference	Cultural Horizon**
Chilcotin Region (continued)						
FcSi 2	Potlatch	C	1615+80	S 500	Wilmeth 1978b	P
"	"	C	1870+75	S 501	" "	P?
"	"	C	130+80	S 923	" "	PH
"	"	C	1695+90	S 945	" "	P?
"	"	C	120+130	GSC 1154	" "	PH
"	"	C	280+170	GSC 1371	" "	K?
FdSi 11	Nakwantlun	C	2400+100	S 1415	Rutherford	?
"	"	C	1870+60	S 1416	et al 1981	?
"	"	C	2410+240	S 1417	" "	?
"	"	C	840+60	S 1446	" "	?
"	"	C	2490+50	S 1589	" "	?
"	"	C	340+50	S 1590	" "	?
"	"	C	430+50	S 1591	" "	?
"	"	C	180+40	S 1592	" "	?
"	"	C	3500+70	S 1593	" "	?
"	"	C	2480+50	S 1594	" "	?
"	"	C	2370+70	S 1608	" "	?
"	"	C	2530+50	S 1609	" "	?
"	"	C	1010+60	S 1610	" "	?
"	"	C	500+45	S 1611	" "	?
"	"	C	880+60	S 1612	" "	?
"	"	C	2500+120	S 1811	Rutherford	?
"	"	C	980+60	S 1812	et al 1984	?
"	"	C	1210+60	S 1813	" "	?
"	"	C	1290+60	S 1995	" "	?
"	"	C	1190+60	S 1996	" "	?
"	"	C	1600+80	S 1998	" "	?
"	"	C	480+70	S 1999	" "	?
"	"	C	1840+280	S 2000	" "	?
"	"	C	1520+160	S 2001	" "	?
FdSi 29	--	C	140+80	SFU 8	Nelson and	PH?
FdSi 31	--	C	230+110	SFU 9	Hobson 1982	PH?

continued

Table 12. (continued)

Site Number	Site Name	Sample Type*	Date (BP)	Lab Number	Reference	Cultural Horizon**
Blackwater River-Southern Nechako Plateau						
FgSd 1	Tezli	C	565+65	S 585	Wilmeth 1978a	K
"	"	C	1870±100	S 586	" "	P?
"	"	C	240±155	S 666	" "	K
"	"	C	3275±405	S 667	" "	S
"	"	C	335±135	S 768	" "	K
"	"	C	3850±140	S 769	" "	S
"	"	C	2335±120	S 770	" "	P
"	"	C	1920±90	S 771	" "	P?
"	"	C	100±60	S 1035	" "	PH
"	"	C	1490±120	Gak 3280	" "	P
FiRs 1	Punchaw Lake	C	560±75	Gak 4905	Fladmark 1976	K
"	" "	C	290±70	Gak 4906	" "	K?
"	" "	C	3980±100	Gak 4907	" "	S?
"	" "	C	250±70	Gak 4908	" "	K?
"	" "	C	1510±100	Gak 6230	Montgomery 1978	P
"	" "	C	1470±100	Gak 6231	" "	P
"	" "	C	240±150	Gak 6232	" "	K
FiSi 19	Natalkuz Lake	C	2415±160	S 4	Wilmeth 1978a	S?
"	" "	C	1950±120	SFU 71	R. Carlson, pers. comm. 1985	?

* C=charcoal; B=bone collagen; W=wood; A=antler collagen.

** S=Shuswap; P=Plateau; K=Kamloops; PH=Protohistoric.

Table 13. Late Prehistoric Canadian Plateau radiocarbon date frequencies plotted by 100-year increments for the Mid-Fraser River region and other regions.

Radiocarbon Years BP	Radiocarbon Date Frequency: Mid-Fraser	Other Regions	Combined
100	0	10	10
200	0	15	15
300	2	4	6
400	0	9	9
500	1	12	13
600	0	3	3
700	1	14	15
800	3	8	11
900	3	4	7
1000	3	6	9
1100	4	8	12
1200	8	12	20
1300	7	2	9
1400	8	6	14
1500	6	3	9
1600	2	6	8
1700	1	3	4
1800	0	4	4
1900	1	10	11
2000	0	4	4
2100	3	3	6
2200	0	3	3
2300	1	3	4
2400	0	6	6
2500	1	5	6
2600	3	2	5
2700	2	0	2
2800	0	1	1
2900	1	2	3
3000	0	2	2
3100	0	3	3
3200	2	3	5
3300	0	0	0
3400	0	0	0
3500	0	1	1
3600	0	0	0
3700	0	0	0
3800	0	1	1
3900	0	3	3
4000	0	0	0